ALL THE PAINTINGS OF
LORENZO LOTTO
Part 2
VOLUME SEVENTEEN
in the
Complete Library of World Art

The Complete Library of World Ar

ALL THE PAINTINGS

OF **LORENZO LOTTO**

Part 2

By PIERO BIANCONI
Translated from the Italian by
PAUL COLACICCHI

OLDBOURNE

London

Printed in Great Britain by
Jarrold and Sons Ltd, Norwich

CONTENTS

LOTTO'S PAINTINGS

THE CREDARO FRESCOES

(Plates 94–97)

In 1525, Lotto frescoed the ceiling, the principal wall, and the two short lateral walls of a small open Chapel attached to the Church of San Giorgio a Credaro (Bergamo). Later, the Chapel was unfortunately turned into a Sacristy and a door was broken through its principal side, damaging the paintings, and the open arches were walled in. On the ledge above the main wall the following words have been discovered: LAURENTIUS LOTUS MDXXV . . . and below *The Nativity* other words beginning EX VOTO . . . but the donor's name has been scraped away.

In the vaulting a ruined but still powerful figure of *God the Father* in green and red is visible (plate 94a).

On the principal wall: *The Nativity with SS Rock and Sebastian* (plate 95). Simple architectural elements in pale yellow on the left, and from the opening on the right appear a few shepherds, a composition that Salvoldo was to use later. The Virgin mantled in a splendid robe of white and gray adores the Infant and St Joseph shows Him to the Saints with a moving gesture. The fresco has suffered badly from time and exposure and the wall on the right of the little door is cracked.

On the right wall: *St Lawrence*, an opulent figure in yellow and gold (plate 96b), turns towards *The Nativity*. In the lunette above him are two *Saints*, perhaps Jerome and Anthony of Padua (plate 96a).

On the left wall: *St George*, extremely elegant in white, wearing a gold chain and holding a mace (plate 97b). Above him are SS *Bartholomew and Catherine of Alexandria* (plate 97a).

The skirtings are in faked marble and the columns and mosaics are also painted. Over the entrance, inside the Church, are sad fragments of an *Archangel Gabriel* and an *Annunciation* described by Berenson in 1905 as "a mere ruin." Over the High Altar: *St George Slaying the Dragon* (plate 94b). Berenson once saw a parallel between Raphael's horse in *The Expulsion of Heliodorus* in the Vatican and a similar animal portrayed by Lotto above the Chapel's entrance and to the right of *The Annunciation*. This horse having disappeared in its entirety, Berenson found (1955) the same affinities between the Raphael and this coarse little picture, some elements of which, however, are fairly typical of Lotto—such as the frantic Princess in the background.

Measurements: *Nativity*, 275 × 310; *St Lawrence* and *St George*, 180 × 80; the two semi-lunettes, 110 × 80; *Archangel Gabriel*, about 120 × 90; *St George Slaying the Dragon*, about 90 × 140.

THE FRESCOES OF SAN MICHELE
AL POZZO BIANCO AT BERGAMO

(Plates 98–103)

Lotto decorated as he had at Credaro the Chapel on the left of the main altar of the Church of San Michele al Pozzo Bianco at Bergamo. The frescoes are signed and dated LAURENTIUS LOTUS MDXXV (just as at Credaro), and they represent scenes from the life of the Virgin. The series was restored in 1928 by M. Pellicioli.

Plate 98

GOD THE FATHER SUPPORTED BY ANGELS. *In the vaulting.* Against a background of sky and clouds.

Plates 99a and b

THE ANNUNCIATION. *On the left lunette, interrupted by the window. About 170 × 230.* The Virgin in white robes is extremely beautiful.

Plate 100

THE BIRTH OF THE VIRGIN. *Central lunette. About 170 × 230.* A tender, almost sad scene, painted in subdued colors; the group on the right, under the rafters, is particularly striking (plate 102). Here Lotto reveals once again his attention to feminine dress.

Plate 101

THE PRESENTATION IN THE TEMPLE and THE MARRIAGE OF THE VIRGIN. *On the right lunette. About 170 × 230.* Here Lotto divided his space into three architectonic views: in the left foreground a group of women watch the child-like Virgin ascending the steps of the Temple where (central section) the High Priest will perform the marriage. At the right Mary's unsuccessful suitors break their staffs rather theatrically. *The Presentation* anticipates the treatment by Tintoretto of the same subject in the Church of Santa Maria dell'Orto in Venice.

Plate 102

THE BIRTH OF THE VIRGIN. Detail: the women on the right.

Plate 103

THE VISITATION. *Over the entrance on the outside of the Chapel. About 170 × 220.* Recent restoration has definitely cleared all remaining controversy about the attribution of this fresco to Lotto. Both figuratively and chromatically the painting is entirely consonant with the Chapel's other decorations. Crowe and Cavalcaselle find in the setting of this *Visitation* "a quiet grandeur and breadth which we do not often meet in Lotto's compositions," and consider all the San Michele frescoes "superior to those of Trescore."

Plate 104

MADONNA NURSING THE CHRIST CHILD. *Panel, 52 × 38. Venice, Museo Correr.* About 1525. In 1901, Berenson expressed doubts about assigning it to Lotto himself, but in his 1955 edition he admits that he "cannot see who else could have done the Madonna and Child but Lotto in one of his most expressive moods." In fact the archaism of this painting is difficult to explain, unless one assumes with Longhi that to please some devoted woman he undertook to copy precisely one of Lazzaro Bastiani's Madonnas.

Plate 105

PORTRAIT OF AN ARCHITECT. *Canvas, 105 × 82. Berlin, Staatliches Museen.* Signed and executed about 1525–30. The date is controversial, as indeed is the subject himself, identified as Sansovino by Crowe and Cavalcaselle but as Sebastiano Serlio by others, probably more correctly. Like the other two Lotto portraits at Berlin (plates 106 and 114), this one was formerly (1815) in the Giustiniani Collection.

Plate 106

PORTRAIT OF A YOUTH AGAINST A GREEN CURTAIN. *Canvas, 47 × 38. Berlin, Staatliches Museen.* Boschetto dates it about 1525–30. Formerly in the Giustiniani Collection.

Plate 107a

SS FRANCIS AND CLARE. *Arched panel, 86 × 152. Jesi, Pinacoteca.* 1526. Lunette of plate 107b. In poor condition. Pallucchini observes that the device of placing St Francis between the light and the spectator anticipates El Greco or Caravaggio's followers.

Plate 107b

MADONNA ENTHRONED WITH SAINTS. *Panel, 152 × 147. Jesi, Pinacoteca.* Signed and dated 1526. Formerly in the Church of San Francesco at Monte. Bald, humpbacked, and aged, St Joseph is a figure of great humanity. Pallucchini stresses the poetic force of details such as the Child's delicate coloring and the rose bush on the window at the left. Note also the rose petals at the foot of the throne. By the Virgin's feet lie St Joseph's water-flask and the cardinal's hat of St Jerome.

Plates 108–09

THE ARCHANGEL GABRIEL and THE ANNUNCIATE VIRGIN. *Panels, 82 × 42 each. Jesi, Pinacoteca.* About 1526. The Angel, suddenly arrested in mid-flight, is a vibrant figure. The Virgin's posture anticipates that of the Recanati *Annunciation* (plate 132). In these last panels (plates 107–09), Pallucchini sees the realization of the "captured moment," a Lotto technique which he began using at Bergamo, inspired by some undefined Northern influences (Grünewald or Altdorfer).

Color Plate V

PORTRAIT OF A DOMINICAN STEWARD. Detail of plate 111.

Plate 110

PORTRAIT OF A YOUNG MAN. *Panel, 35 × 28. Milan, Castello Sforzesco. Formerly in the De Cristoforis Collection.* About 1526. Restored by Cavenaghi. A surprisingly modern work: the black stripes on the grayish lilac coat, seen against a green ground, have reminded some critics of Manet. Observe the counterpoint of the young man's hands, one gloved, one bare, holding a well-thumbed book. The portrait, one of Lotto's best, offers an interesting psychological insight in the cold, remote and vaguely sulking expression of the face.

Plate 111

PORTRAIT OF A DOMINICAN STEWARD. *Canvas, 78 × 68. Treviso, Pinacoteca.* Signed and dated 1526. Bequeathed to the Pinacoteca by the nobleman Sernagiotto. Thought to be a Steward of the Convent of San Giovanni e Paolo at Venice, painted shortly after Lotto's return to that city. Note the admirable still life of coins, papers, keys, and votive candles.

Plate 112

PORTRAIT OF A DOMINICAN STEWARD. Detail: the hands and still life.

Plate 113

MADONNA IN LANDSCAPE WITH TWO DONORS. *Canvas, 89 × 114. Formerly in the Palazzo Rospigliosi, Rome, and until recently in the W. R. Hearst Collection, New York.* Longhi believes the Madonna to have been painted from a drawing by Giulio Romano; Coletti thinks the two donors to have been reproduced from a painting by Palma and submits the theory that Lotto may have completed a work started by Palma. Both Coletti and Fiocco date the canvas 1529.

Plate 114

BUST OF A YOUTH AGAINST A RED CURTAIN. *Canvas, 47 × 39. Berlin, Staatliches Museen.* Signed. Executed about 1526. Thought by some to be a self-portrait. Berenson remarks "This portrait may be called Lotto's 'Homme au gant.' It has the masterly directness and simplicity of that great Titian but it is not so impersonal, is more sensitive, more intellectual—an Italian of the first part of the sixteenth century, who belongs to neither of the varieties catalogued by Stendhal and all the other writers . . . the young man before us is neither cut-throat nor artist."

Plate 115

THE ASSUMPTION OF THE VIRGIN. *Canvas, 250 × 210. Celana (Bergamo), Church of Santa Maria Assunta.* Signed and dated 1527. One of Lotto's happiest creations, with the mannered fluttering of robes, ribbons, and wings, the play of light, the chorus of Apostles whose excitement is expressed by the striking counterpoint of hands against the landscape. In the group to the right some have recognized Lotto himself, the jeweler, Bartolomeo Carpan, and the architect, Zuan dal Coro from Ancona. Both men are frequently mentioned in the "Book of Accounts."

THE PONTERANICA POLYPTYCH

(Plates 116–19)

This altarpiece, composed of six panels, is in the Church of Santi Vincenzo e Alessandro at Ponteranica (Bergamo). Signed and dated 1527, but the date is not perfectly clear, for the last number is erased. The subjects and measurements of the six panels are: *The Redeemer,* arched panel, *135 × 70* (plate 116b); *St John the Baptist,* arched panel, *135 × 70* (plate 117a); *St Peter,* arched panel, *118 × 87* (plate 116a); *St Paul,* arched panel, *118 × 87* (plate 117b); *The Archangel Gabriel,* panel, *75 × 35* (plate 118), and *The Annunciate Virgin,* panel, *75 × 35* (plate 119). Berenson does not think this work

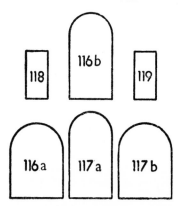

entirely Lotto's—the figures of *The Redeemer* and *St Peter* are doubtful—but considers *Gabriel* "the loveliest angel Lotto has left us." *The Redeemer*, with the blood spurting from His wounds into a chalice at His feet, reminds Zampetti of Lotto's contacts with German art and especially with Grünewald. The Lamb in St John the Baptist's arms is also bleeding.

Plate 120

THE NATIVITY. *Panel, 45 × 30. Siena, Pinacoteca*. Executed about 1527, signed. At one time considered a seventeenth-century copy of a Flemish master, but published as a work by Lotto by Fiocco in 1934 and Ciaranfi in 1936. This attribution is now universally accepted. Coletti draws attention to the midwife's clenched hands. Lotto loved the ancient theme, as he described it, of "a Nativity by night, and the radiance emanating from Christ casting light all round" and painted many versions of it. The colors of this panel are magnificent and enamel-like, some details like the copper vases on the right prefigure Bassano.

Plate 121

MAN ON A TERRACE. *Canvas, 110 × 102. Cleveland (Ohio), Museum of Art*. Signed and dated 15 . . . ; reasonably assumed to have been executed about 1527, though Berenson (1955) favors the date 1525. Formerly in the Ofenheim Collection at Vienna. The dramatic gesticulation of this rather vain figure is generally not consonant with Lotto's more modest subjects. On this occasion the artist has replaced his beloved rose petals with a branch of jasmine.

Plate 122

PORTRAIT OF BISHOP TOMMASO NEGRI. *Panel, 42 × 54. Split, Monastero delle Paludi*. Signed and dated 1527. Published by G. De Nicola in 1908. Described by Banti as a "pre-Rembrandt Oracle." Berenson published in 1955 a *Head of a Bearded Prelate* (see *Lorenzo Lotto*, Phaidon Press, plate 216), the facial features of which are strikingly similar to those of Bishop Negri.

Plate 123

PORTRAIT OF ANDREA ODONI. *Canvas, 114 × 101. Hampton Court, Royal Gallery*. Signed and dated 1527. Seen by Vasari and Michiel in the house of Odoni at Venice, the stateliness of which was described in a letter by Aretino, in 1538. This superb portrait, highly praised by Crowe and Cavalcaselle, is analogous to the so-called *Lucretia* (plate 136). (See also plate 124.)

Plate 124

PORTRAIT OF ANDREA ODONI. Detail: statue on the left. From an indication of Professor Giovanni Becatti, Berenson identifies the original from which this piece of sculpture was copied as a fragmentary group of Hercules and Antaeus that stood in the Belvedere Courtyard of the Vatican during Lotto's lifetime.

Plate 125

GENTLEMAN HOLDING A GOLDEN CLAW. *Canvas, 97 × 71. Vienna, Kunsthistorisches Museum*. About 1527. This noble figure stands in front of a scarlet curtain sharply lighted from the left, and leans against a table covered with a green cloth. He gives an impression of uncertainty and instability. Face and hands stand out from the flowing dark mantle and the brown garb trimmed with turquoise-blue; his right hand rests on his heart, and in his left he holds a golden hare's foot. This has led some critics to suppose that the sitter may have been a jeweler. One of Lotto's finest portraits.

Color Plate VI
THE NATIVITY. Detail of plate 120.

Plate 126
YOUNG MAN IN HIS STUDY. *Canvas, 98 × 111. Venice, Gallerie dell'Accademia.* About 1527. Formerly in the Rovere house at Treviso, where Coletti discovered it in 1923. It is a searching portrait that proves Lotto's capacity for understatement. In the background we see a hunting-horn, a cap with a medal, a dead bird. The young man sits at his desk in front of a large open book and from the folds of the desk cover, among the petals of roses, a green lizard is watching him (plate 127). The pale hands emerging from the lace cuffs, frame this beautiful still life. The date of execution is controversial: Coletti (1953) suggested 1515 because of the affinity with the portrait of the Della Torre brothers (plate 35b), but probably Lotto painted it near the end of the Bergamo period. (See also plates 127–28.)

Plate 127
YOUNG MAN IN HIS STUDY. Detail: still life.

Plate 128
YOUNG MAN IN HIS STUDY. Detail: the face.

Plate 129
THE ADORATION OF THE SHEP-HERDS. *Canvas, 147 × 166. Brescia, Pinacoteca Tosio-Martinengo.* About 1527–28. The scene retains a pleasing touch of Italian rustic theater and of *sacra rappresentazione*, thus confirming the traditional belief that the Virgin and the Angels were modeled from the wife and daughters of one of the Gussoni brothers who are seen here in the role of shepherds. There is something of a posed Christmas portrait of a family in this picture; the shepherds especially, as remarked by Berenson, have portrait features. The pictorial invention is striking: the blending of muted yellows, browns, blacks, and whites; the back-lighting which silhouettes Joseph, the Angel, and the donkey creates another plane, anticipating Savoldo, while the full lighting in the fore-ground, anticipates Caravaggio. (See also plate 130.)

Plate 130
THE ADORATION OF THE SHEP-HERDS. Detail: the Child and a lamb.

Plate 131
SACRA CONVERSAZIONE. *Canvas, 113 × 152. Vienna, Kunsthistorisches Museum.* About 1527–29. Recorded by Boschini (*Carta del Navegar Pitoresco*) in the Collection of the Austrian Emperor. In this passage, written in Venetian dialect and in verse, Lotto is called: "That famous Bergamasco and rare imitator of Palma Vecchio." The chromatic consonance of this canvas is truly exceptional: the liquid blue, for instance, of the Virgin's robe and the Angel's pink and purple. Lights and shadows run swiftly through this group heightening the open-air atmosphere. Lotto was about fifty years old when he achieved this

incomparable clarity in his expression.

Plate 132

THE ANNUNCIATION. *Canvas, 166 × 114. Recanati, Church of Santa Maria sopra Mercanti.* Signed and datable about 1527-29. A pale northern light filters into the room from the little window; the detail in the domestic background contrasts with the rather awkward figure of God the Father hovering above the parapet. An intense dialogue seems to be going on between the flaxen-haired Angel in blue and the awed Virgin. Note the terrified cat, whose function in the composition is that of linking the figures of Mary and the messenger.

Plate 133

ST NICHOLAS OF BARI IN GLORY. *Canvas, rounded top, 335 × 188. Venice, Church of the Carmini.* Signed and dated 1529 (Ridolfi), and mentioned by Vasari, this canvas marks the time when Lotto's art came closest to that of Titian, a development for which he was ill-rewarded, as this work was bitterly criticized by Dolce (*Dialogo*, 1557): "A remarkable example of these bad hues can be seen, in my opinion, in a painting by Lorenzo Lotto here in Venice in the Carmini Church." In fact the best features of this altarpiece—Lotto's first public commission in Venice—are to be found not in its upper part, which is rather cumbersome, but in the beautiful landscape below (plate 134): "a wide stretch of landscape, with a view of the sea from inland, paths winding down to a port, and travelers going toward the coast. In the foreground to the right, St George fights the Dragon while the Princess flees towards a castle" (Berenson). (See also plate 134.)

Plate 134

ST NICHOLAS OF BARI IN GLORY. Detail: the landscape.

Plate 135

PORTRAIT OF A MAN IN THREE POSITIONS. *Canvas, 52 × 79. Vienna, Kunsthistorisches Museum.* About 1530-35. Formerly in the Collection of Charles I and attributed to Titian, as reported by Crowe and Cavalcaselle who assigned it to Lotto in 1891. Wickoff (1893) sees in this model the St James in the *Sacra Conversazione* (plate 131) also at Vienna. Kerr-Lawson, on the other hand, believes it to be a self-portrait. This assumption is based on a pun on Lotto's name if the rings in the box are tokens from the game of *lotto*, in the center foreground. This theory met with some success and Biagi went so far as to state that the central figure is actually pointing to himself, as if to say: "It's me." This is confirmed by Coletti and other critics. From the rings, however, one could be tempted to identify the sitter with Lorenzo's jeweler friend, Bartolomeo Carpan. However, the theory of a self-portrait is not unattractive, and Longhi has recently given it further support by connecting it to the figure of the philosopher Aeschines in Raphael's *School of Athens* fresco in the Vatican. This, if proved, would provide important evidence for the belief that Lotto collaborated with Raphael in decorating the *Stanze*, as claimed by Longhi in a lecture given at Venice in October 1953.

Plate 136

PORTRAIT OF A LADY AS LUCRETIA. *Canvas, 95 × 110. London, National Gallery.* About 1528-30. Formerly in the Holford Collection where it was catalogued as a Giorgione. First attributed to Lotto by Morelli. The woman, standing between an empty cradle—which Berenson now describes as a "savonarola chair"—and a table, is wearing a red-and-white turban and a dress of brownish-red striped with green; she is pointing to a drawing of Lucretia. A piece of paper on the table bears the inscription: "*Nec ulla impudica Lucretiae exemplo vivet*," whence the name of *Lucretia* traditionally given to the portrait, and the assumption that the sitter was a courtesan. The Latin inscription (from Livy, I, 58) means: "No woman shall lead a life of shame in future if she recalls Lucretia's example."

Plate 137

THE ALLEGORY OF CHASTITY. *Canvas, 76 × 118. Rome, Rospigliosi-Pallavicini Collection.* Signed and datable about 1530. Formerly attributed to Luca Cambiaso. Morelli would have it painted in the Bergamo period. The nude Venus is so cold that Coletti recalls the work of Canova and Berenson (1955) is reminded of a nude on a sarcophagus in the Vatican. In contrast, an angry Chastity is a mass of ruffles. Venus holds on her shoulder a beautiful casket with combs and other toilet articles. (See also plate 138.)

Plate 138

THE ALLEGORY OF CHASTITY. Detail: head of Chastity.

Plate 139

PORTRAIT OF A GENTLEMAN DRESSED IN BLACK. *Canvas, 118 × 105. Rome, Borghese Gallery.* About 1530. Formerly attributed to Pordenone and assigned to Lotto in 1869 by Mundler. One of Lotto's most typical paintings: a dark, sad figure, with one hand pressed to his side as if in pain and the other

resting on a tiny skull bedded in rose and jasmine petals (plate 141). Through the open window a town can be seen with hills beyond, and a small *St George Slaying the Dragon* (plate 140), treated similarly to the one in the Carmini Church at Venice. St Nicholas or St George could have been the patron of the sitter. Other scholars, among them P. Della Pergola, submit that this is a self-portrait. (See also plates 140–41.)

Plate 140

PORTRAIT OF A GENTLEMAN DRESSED IN BLACK. Detail: landscape on the left.

Plate 141

PORTRAIT OF A GENTLEMAN DRESSED IN BLACK. Detail: the hand and still life.

Plate 142

CHRIST AND THE ADULTERESS. *Canvas, 124 × 156. Paris, Louvre.* About 1530. As in the *Madonna and Child with Saints* (plate 17) the composition, the display of hands, and the faces in this scene strongly recall Dürer and Lucas van Leyden. There is a fascinating contrast between the course features of the Pharisees and the serenity in the face of Christ; between the man in armor and the tender woman, softly shaped and adorned with pearls. An inferior replica (canvas, 105 × 132), painted later and possibly in the workshop, still exists at Loreto, but has been totally ruined by a restorer (Berenson and Gianuizzi). In 1540, Lotto was painting yet another version of this subject for Messer Zuan Donà Usper.

Plate 143

APOLLO ASLEEP ON PARNASSUS. *Canvas, 45.5 × 75. Budapest, Museum* of Fine Arts (Study Department). About 1530. Published by A. Pigler and Berenson, who dated it (in 1955) "at the end of Lotto's Bergamo period or soon afterwards." Mentioned in the "Book of Accounts" among the works auctioned by Lotto at Ancona in 1550.

Plate 144

MALE PORTRAIT. *Canvas, 74 × 60. Milan, Crespi Collection.* About 1530–35. The attribution, by M. Pellicioli, is endorsed by Boschetto, Coletti, and Berenson. Whatever doubts still exist about the authorship are due to some rather lifeless outlines, which Lotto normally drew with great vivacity.

Plate 145a

THE ANNUNCIATION. *Canvas, rounded top, 103 × 52 (lunette of* The Visitation *on following plate). Jesi, Pinacoteca.* About 1530.

Plate 145b

THE VISITATION. *Canvas, 154 × 152. Jesi, Pinacoteca.* Signed and dated 1530 (?). Previously in the Church of San Francesco at Monte, the property of the Zoccolanti Friars. Pallucchini states that the date is not 1530—as traditionally read—but some years later. The tones are cold and dense; the composition is monumental with great pathos. The pregnant old woman, in black and purple, dominates the scene. The mantel in the background is very similar to that of the Recanati *Annunciation* (plate 132); upon it fruit and household objects are vividly depicted. The ground is strewn with violets. In 1955 Berenson published a *Drawing for the Jesi Visitation.* (See also plate 146.)

Plate 146

THE VISITATION. Detail: Zachariah and Elizabeth.

Plate 147

CHRIST ON THE CROSS WITH THE SYMBOLS OF THE PASSION. *Convex panel, 18 × 14.5. Florence, Berenson Collection.* About 1530. Formerly in the Borromeo Collection in Milan. On the reverse is the following translated inscription:

> "*This picture is by the hand of Messer Lorenzo Lotto, a most devout man who, as a spiritual exercise, painted it during the Holy Week and finished it on Good Friday at the hour of the Passion of our Lord Jesus Christ. I, Zanetto del Co. have written this in order that it may be known to all and that this painting may be held in the veneration that it deserves.*"

We may assume that the inscription was by the architect from Ancona, Zuan del Coro, a close friend of Lotto. Both the picture and the writing reveal the artist's deep religious feelings. In this context one should not forget the copy of a portrait of Luther and his wife painted by Lotto in Venice in 1540. Berenson is right in stating that in Lotto: "What is ancient and what is new coexist peacefully, in separate layers, with no antagonism or contradiction."

Plate 148

THE CRUCIFIXION. *Canvas, arched top, 450 × 250. Monte San Giusto, (Macerata), Church of Santa Maria in Telusiano.* Signed and dated 1531. Preserved in its magnificent original frame, this canvas is considered by Berenson to be one of Lotto's major pieces, conceived "in the spirit of a Greek tragedy." On the left, an Angel with outstretched arms shows the fainting Virgin to the donor, Bishop of Chiusi, Niccolò Bonafede. In the background, against a dramatic sky, the three white crosses have the appearance of pale phantoms: the draperies of the three crucified men "stream out against the clouds" (Berenson); on Christ's right the good thief seems to be walking on air toward the Redeemer, and the unrepenting one turns his face away into the shadows; below the crosses, on the high ground a lively scene of men and horses, of spears and standards, and of forceful gesturing —the portraits bearing a strong resemblance to those of *The St Lucy Altarpiece* (plate 154). In the foreground the Virgin has fainted into the arms of St John and Mary Magdalen expresses her grief with frantic gestures. The whole effect is grandiose and three-dimensional, framed and organized by light which reconciles the incongruous perspectives and the arbitrary relationships which we often find in Lotto—here, the one between the Angel and the donor, and the central group. These, however, are critical observations; ultimately, the artist's expressive powers, the magnificent passion which he has given this great canvas have created a poetic reality whose effectiveness is beyond argument. A copy by Simone da Caldarola still exists in the Pinacoteca at Matelica. (See also plates 149–51.)

Plate 149

THE CRUCIFIXION. Detail: the good thief.

Plate 150

THE CRUCIFIXION. Detail: a horseman at left.

Plate 151

THE CRUCIFIXION. Detail: women at right.

Plates 152a and b

ST SEBASTIAN and ST CHRISTOPHER. *Two canvases framed together*: *139 × 55 each. Berlin, Staatliches Museen.* Signed and dated 1531. Formerly (1821) in the Solly Collection. These are probably reminders of a more complex work, such as the later treatment of the same subject at Loreto (see following plate). Here there is a striking contrast between the almost feminine beauty of St Sebastian and the herculean St Christopher.

Plate 153

SS ROCK, CHRISTOPHER, AND SEBASTIAN. *Panel, 275 × 232. Loreto, Palazzo Apostolico.* Signed and datable about 1532–34. The designs for the two Saints in the previous plate were used again here in a pyramidal composition. Frizzoni draws attention to a fascinating detail: "a little snake's head and tail protruding out of a rolled up piece of paper upon which a human eye is drawn in perspective," and the artist's signature. Details such as these will reappear in the canvases of El Greco.

Plate 154

THE ST LUCY ALTARPIECE. *Panel, 243 × 237. Jesi, Pinacoteca.* Signed and dated 1532. Formerly in the Church of San Floriano. Lotto received the order for this work from the Confraternità di Santa Lucia at Jesi as far back as December 11, 1523. He was urged to finish it in 1527 and in 1528, but only when the Order threatened to transfer the commission to Giuliano Presutti of Fano did he complete the painting, the last payment for which was made on February 5, 1531. The main force in the picture is once again the light, treated in much the same way as in the altarpiece in the Carmini Church: it comes from the left through the portico, brushing the hand and knee of the seated tyrant, highlighting the small boy in the foreground who strains to escape from the arms of his nurse (plate 155) and playing fully on the Saint, dressed in red and yellow. Around the figure of Lucy flash the colors of the executioners and accusers, and a crowd of faces stares from the background. In spite of its virtues, something crude and harsh can still be detected in this altarpiece, and it compares unfavorably with its beautiful predella reproduced in plates 156–58. (See also plate 155.)

Plate 155

THE ST LUCY ALTARPIECE. Detail: the nurse and child.

Plates 156–58

SCENES FROM THE LEGEND OF ST LUCY. *Three panels, 32 × 69 each, forming the predella of the above altarpiece. Jesi, Pinacoteca.* About 1530. As remarked by Coletti, the episodes should be read as follows: 1. *St Lucy at the Tomb of St Agatha* (plate 156); 2. *St Lucy before the Judges* (plate 157); 3. *St Lucy Arguing with the Judges* (*The St Lucy Altarpiece*, plate 154); 4. *St Lucy Condemned and the Miracle of the Vain Attempt to Drag Her Away* (plate 158). Lotto's light was perhaps never as mobile as on the walls and niches of the Bramantesque architecture in these panels, where we see the Saint sleeping by the altar, hearing Mass and giving alms. Light is used by the master to create space amid the waving pikes and standard and the train of oxen, finally opening a background not to be seen again until the atmospheric paintings of the nineteenth century. The narrative energy recalls the Trescore frescoes. (See also plates 159a and b.)

Plate 159a

SCENES FROM THE LEGEND OF ST LUCY. Detail: niche with the *ex voto* offerings in the first panel.

Plate 159b

SCENES FROM THE LEGEND OF ST LUCY. Detail: two oxen in the third panel.

Plate 160

PORTRAIT OF A GENTLEMAN. *Canvas, 94 × 82. New Orleans, Delgado Museum of Art (S. H. Kress Collection).* About 1532–33. Formerly in the Giovanelli Collection at Venice. In 1946 Longhi dated it about 1546.

Plate 161

HOLY FAMILY WITH ST CATHERINE. *Canvas, 81 × 115. Bergamo, Accademia Carrara.* Signed and dated 1533. In 1632, this picture was part of the Collection of Roberto Canonici at Ferrara. Crowe and Cavelcaselle admire its chromatic scale of pearl and iron grays, of greens and reds. There is also a remarkable coherence of curves and vigorous movements, and enchanting counterpoint in the fig and jasmine leaves. Several replicas exist: at Houston, Texas, in the Osmitz Collection at Pressburg (Bratislava), and at the Hermitage in Leningrad. Pietro Zampetti has published (*Arte Veneta*, 1956, p. 185) a version signed and dated 1529, in a private collection near Bergamo. That version should therefore be considered as the original treatment of this composition.

Plate 162

VIRGIN AND CHILD WITH SS ANNE, JOACHIM, AND JEROME. *Canvas, 67 × 85. Florence, Uffizi.* Signed and dated 1534. Agitated movements and forms, and cold colors, mark this work. Berenson, who describes it as being "of unequal quality," published (1955) another version of it, with a landscape in place of St Jerome, in the Collection of Count Antoine Seilern at London.

Plate 163

THE RECOGNITION OF THE HOLY CHILD. *Canvas, 150 × 237. Paris, Louvre.* About 1535. Cavalcaselle considered it an unfinished Lotto. Boschetto believes it to be a replica of the same subject as painted at Loreto (plate 203); this is contrary to current opinion, though Boschetto admits that the quality of this canvas is superior. The composition is lively, exclamatory and daring in the arrangement of colors: blue and pink on the right, brick-red and yellow on the left.

Plate 164a

ST ANTHONY THE HERMIT. *Panel, 34 × 41. Wilton House, Salisbury, Collection of the Earl of Pembroke and Montgomery.* About 1534. Fiocco sees the influence of Dürer in this picture. Berenson states that the head of the Saint is almost certainly a portrait.

Plate 164b

ST JEROME IN THE WILDERNESS. *Canvas, 91 × 75. Venice, Private Collection.* Signed and datable about 1535–40. Discovered by Rodolfo Pallucchini if one believes Boschetto, but the Catalogue of the Venice Exhibition assigns the discovery to Fiocco. One of Lotto's Titianesque works.

Plate 165

MADONNA WITH SLEEPING CHILD. *Canvas, 67 × 55. Sarasota, Florida, Ringling Museum of Art.* About 1535. Suida states that in his view this work was painted in the last years of the master's life. Berenson notes that the motif of the sleeping Child is the same as that in the Carrara Academy at Bergamo (plate 161) and remarks that the Bellinesque composition "harks back to the Quattrocento."

Plate 166

PORTRAIT OF A MAN AGED THIRTY-SEVEN. *Canvas, 95 × 80. Rome, Doria Gallery.* About 1535–40. On the ivy-covered wall is a stone with the inscription: ANN. AETATIS / SUE / XXXVII; to the left is a bas-relief of a little winged Cherub balancing himself on a pair of scales. The same allegorical figure occurs in the Bergamo *Intarsias*. This work, too, has been considered as a self-portrait, though the chronology would appear to invalidate such a theory. This distressed figure, obviously in great pain, is among the most moving examples of Lotto's vision of a sorrowful humanity.

Plate 167

PORTRAIT OF A GENTLEMAN. *Canvas, 70 × 56.7. Venice, Cini Collection.* Formerly in the Heimann Collection at New York, and originally in the house of Count Avogadro of Treviso (Coletti), this may be a portrait mentioned in Lotto's "Book of Accounts" in October 1542. Berenson calls this work: *Portrait of Girolamo degli Azzoni Avogadro.*

Plate 168

THE RECOGNITION OF THE HOLY CHILD. Formerly in the Town Hall at Osimo, from where it was stolen in 1911. See "Lost Paintings."

Plate 169

THE MADONNA OF THE ROSARY. *Canvas, curved top, 384 × 264. Cingoli (Macerata), Church of San Domenico.* Signed and dated 1539. In this unusual composition Lotto returns to his theme of popular piety, as shown in the rose hedge from the branches of which hang, like Japanese lanterns (Berenson), fifteen roundels each one containing a Mystery of the Rosary. The overall effect betrays slight tiredness, but the group of the Infant St John and the two Cherubs scattering rose petals from a wicker basket is delightful (plate 170). To the right, the patron of Cingoli, St Esuperanzio, is offering the Child a model of the town. Tradition has it that the features of Mary Magdalen, on the extreme left, are those of the donor, Sperandia Franceschini Simonetti. The iconography of the roundels is a series of frank and quick sketches. (See also plates 170–73.)

Plate 170

THE MADONNA OF THE ROSARY. Detail: the Infant St John the Baptist and two cherubs scattering rose petals.

Plate 171

THE MADONNA OF THE ROSARY. Details: the Mysteries: *The Annunciation*; *The Visitation*; *The Nativity*.

Plate 172

THE MADONNA OF THE ROSARY. Details: the Mysteries: *The Circumcision*; *Christ Among the Doctors*; *The Agony in the Garden*; *Christ at the Column*; *The Crowning with Thorns*; *Christ Falling under the Cross*.

Plate 173

THE MADONNA OF THE ROSARY. Details: the Mysteries: *The Crucifixion*; *The Resurrection*; *The Ascension*; *The Descent of the Holy Spirit*; *The Assumption*; *The Coronation of the Virgin*. Of the last-named scene Berenson wrote: "Lotto attains here a sublimity which is rare elsewhere in painting and which I can compare to Milton only."

Color Plate VII

PORTRAIT OF LAURA DA POLA. Detail of plate 183.

Plate 174

MADONNA ENTHRONED WITH FOUR SAINTS. *Canvas, 294 × 216. Ancona, Church of Santa Maria della Piazza.* Signed and datable about 1540–46. Formerly in the Church of Sant'Agostino, where it was seen by Vasari. The accented light and shade anticipates Caravaggio; the coloring is like Titian's. Pallucchini, having stressed the picture's monumental grandeur, remarks that the figures "appear in the light and disappear in a most delicate half-shadow." A preparatory drawing for St Joseph, seen in the foreground to the right, is in the Collection of Mrs Julia Rayner-Wood at Malvern.

Plate 175

ST ANTONINUS ALTARPIECE. *Canvas, curved top, 332 × 235. Venice, Church of San Giovanni e Paolo.* Signed and executed in 1542 for the sum of one hundred and twenty-five ducats (thirty-five of which were put aside for Lotto's burial). As often in Lotto's works, the best features of this work are not in its upper part, that is in the sacred representation, necessarily traditional, but in the lower half, where the master's invention and freedom of action found fuller scope. The two deacons behind the parapet —one distributing money, the other receiving petitions—are persuasive portraits, and in the "Book of Accounts" of that period several entries refer to small payments made "in order to portray the poor." The crowd of beggars below the parapet had been compared by Longhi to similar scenes by Goya. Berenson had previously observed that Lotto, with a dozen heads, can produce the effect of multitudes, so compelling is his feeling for movement. (See also plates 176–78.)

Plate 176

ST ANTONINUS ALTARPIECE. Detail: the deacon on the right.

Plate 177

ST ANTONINUS ALTARPIECE. Detail: the deacon on the left.

Plate 178

ST ANTONINUS ALTARPIECE. Detail: women at the center.

Plate 179

ST JEROME IN THE WILDERNESS. *Canvas, 51 × 43. Rome, Doria Gallery.* About 1540–45. Formerly attributed to one of the Carracci brothers.

Plate 180

VIRGIN IN GLORY WITH SAINTS. *Canvas, 310 × 210. Sedrina (Bergamo), Parish Church.* Signed and dated: HOC OPUS FECIT FIERI FRATERNITAS SANTE MARIE DE SEDRINA 1542. Lotto notes in the "Book of Accounts" that the altarpiece was ordered by a group of wine merchants from Sedrina who promised to pay him fifty gold *scudi*. Beyond the four Saints, who seem to be performing a ritual dance below the celestial vision, is a view of the Brembana valley, with a river and a flock of sheep. The wine merchants must have insisted that this landscape be included in the picture, as identification.

Plate 181

ST FELIX. *Canvas, 139 × 57. Giovanazzo (Bari), Church of San Domenico.* 1542. In the "Book of Accounts" for June 16, 1542, Lotto states that he has undertaken to paint for the above Church a triptych of St Felix between St Anthony of Padua and St Nicholas of Tolentino, surmounted by a lunette with a suffering Christ. The work was to cost thirty ducats but, on being paid

at the end of the year, the master complains in his book that the painting is worth at least sixty ducats, and that he had undertaken to do it in the hope of its value being acknowledged. The two wings and the lunette are lost, but in 1897, Berenson discovered the central canvas in a dustheap at the back of the High Altar of San Domenico. Titianesque and yet modern, the Saint appears encased like a mummy within the narrow canvas.

Plate 182

PORTRAIT OF MESSER FEBO DA BRESCIA. *Canvas, 91 × 77. Milan, Brera Gallery.* Signed 1543. This and the following portrait of Laura da Pola were obviously a pair. Both were formerly in the Harrache (?) Collection at Turin, and were donated to the Brera Gallery in 1860 by King Victor Emmanuel II. Lotto, who was paid little more than thirty ducats for both portraits, complains in the "Book of Accounts" that "it is not even enough to pay for the time employed in the work." Febo's figure is splendidly painted in a kind of monochrome; each part is brought to life by the play of light.

Plate 183

PORTRAIT OF LAURA DA POLA. *Canvas, 91 × 77. Milan, Brera Gallery.* Signed 1543. For the painting's history see comment on plate 182. Though the woman's face is rather expressionless, this is still a magnificent portrait, particularly notable in the richness of Laura's dress, and for her hands, one holding an ostrich-plume fan, the other a book. Crowe and Cavalcaselle praise the picture's rich and colored shadows.

Plate 184

PORTRAIT OF AN OLD MAN. *Canvas, 90 × 75. Milan, Brera Gallery.*

Signed and datable about 1542–44. Perhaps Lotto's greatest achievement in the field of portrait-painting. Its subtlety and firmness are unrivaled.

Plate 185

PORTRAIT OF A MAN WITH SYMBOLS. *Canvas, 99 × 78. El Paso, Texas, Museum of Art (S. H. Kress Collection).* Formerly in the A. W. Spender Collection at Vevey, recalled by Coletti in a private collection at Milan. Executed about 1540–44, though Coletti favors the earlier date of 1527–29. Boschetto describes it with different measurements (108 × 80). This work was exhibited in 1940 at Toledo (Ohio). At one time it was also the property of Sir Charles Robinson, of London, who provided the following interpretation of the symbols as related by Berenson: 1. Deflated bladder = poverty; 2. Pearl with sapphires = wealth; 3. Ox-head = labor; 4. Armillary sphere = worldly renown; 5. Crossed palm branches = fame; 6. Full-blown bladder = notoriety.

Plate 186

PORTRAIT OF AN ELDERLY GENTLEMAN. *Canvas, 115 × 98. Milan, Brera Gallery.* Signed and datable about 1544. Donated to the Gallery in 1855 as part of the Oddoni Bequest. Arcangeli comments on the man's "dark look," the face reflecting an exhausted heart.

Plate 187

CHRIST IN GLORY WITH THE SYMBOLS OF THE PASSION. *Panel, 49 × 33. Vienna, Kunsthistorisches Museum.* About 1543. Some scholars connect this painting with an entry in the "Book of Accounts" for 1543 in which Lotto describes "a small picture of the triumph of Our Savior Jesus in the act of shedding His Blood. He is to be seen high in the Heavens, with many Angels." The description seems to fit the composition perfectly. Yet one has doubts as to whether Lotto could have painted this panel, for it seems more the work of a Mannerist from Emilia influenced by Correggio, to whom it was actually attributed until Frizzoni assigned it to Lotto in 1911. The composition was inspired by a bas-relief by Sansovino in the Church of San Marco in Venice.

Plate 188

PORTRAIT OF THE SURGEON STUER WITH HIS SON. *Canvas, 85 × 72. Philadelphia, J. G. Johnson Collection.* 1544. The "Book of Accounts" states that Stuer ordered the portrait at Treviso in March 1544, and that no contract was made. As usual, his conclusion is a mortifying one: "I had to be content with what he decided to give me."

Plate 189

PIETÀ. *Canvas, 185 × 150. Milan, Brera Gallery.* Signed 1545. The "Book of Accounts" states that on February 10, 1545, the Nuns of San Paolo at Treviso commissioned from Lotto a "small altarpiece of the *Pietà* with the fainting Virgin supported by St John and the dead Christ in His Mother's arms, and with two small Angels supporting His head and feet." The price agreed upon was sixteen ducats.

Color Plate VIII

ST JEROME IN THE WILDERNESS. Detail of plate 190.

Plate 190

ST JEROME IN THE WILDERNESS. *Panel, 99 × 90. Madrid, Prado.* About 1545. Formerly in the Escorial and ascribed to Titian. Berenson believes it to be a larger variant, with the addition of an Angel, of the canvas in the Doria Gallery (see plate 179).

Plate 191

MADONNA ENTHRONED WITH FOUR SAINTS. *Canvas, curved top, 421 × 170. Venice, Church of San Giacomo dell'Orio.* Signed and dated 1546. A hasty replica, showing signs of fatigue, of the Ancona altarpiece (plate 174). Mentioned in the "Book of Accounts" as "an oil-painting of the Virgin and Child, with SS James Andrew, Cosmas and Damian and two small Angels above crowning the Virgin." The price paid was twenty ducats.

Plate 192

CHRIST AT EMMAUS. *Canvas, 74 × 98. Oxford, Christ Church Library.* About 1546. The attribution is by Berenson who refers to a note in the "Book of Accounts" for April 1545: "For Alessandro Catanio, a druggist, a small picture of Christ at Emmaus."

Plate 193

VIRGIN AND CHILD WITH ZACHARIAS AND ST JOHN THE BAPTIST. *Canvas, 48 × 63.5. Milan, Poldi-Pezzoli Museum.* About 1545. Another tired work, and there are still some doubts about its authorship. A replica—published by Boschetto and exhibited at Venice—is in the Basevi Collection at Genoa.

Plate 194

ST MARK IN PRAYER. *Mosaic, 220 × 160. Venice, Atrium of San Marco.* Dated 1545. Formerly assigned to Titian and attributed to Lotto by Longhi in 1947. Longhi's theory has been generally accepted though Berenson notes that it may be valid "if the inevitable alteration due to transporting a drawing into

mosaic is taken into account." Berenson, however, rejects two other designs for mosaics in the Atrium of San Marco, attributed to Lotto by Muraro (see "Attributed Works").

Plate 195

PORTRAIT OF A DOMINICAN FRIAR AS ST PETER MARTYR. *Canvas, 88 × 68. Cambridge, Massachusetts, Fogg Art Museum.* Signed and datable about 1548–49. Though Venturi dates it earlier—in or about 1523—this canvas would appear consistent with the following entry in the "Book of Accounts" for October 1548: "Friar Giovanni Andrea, of the Church of SS Giovanni e Paolo, for his portrait with the attributes of St Peter Martyr;" a similar entry occurs at Ancona the following year. However, this is definitely a portrait, and of a very firm solidity, as visible especially in the impressive concreteness of the right sleeve.

Plate 196

MADONNA IN GLORY WITH SAINTS. *Canvas, curved top, 330 × 215. Mogliano (Macerata), Parish Church.* Signed and datable 1547–48. The "Book of Accounts" shows that on November 16, 1547, Lotto received from Jacopo Boninfanti of Mogliano the order to paint, for the price of one hundred and thirty ducats, an altarpiece and to provide "the wooden and gilded ornaments" for it; on February 6, 1548, Lotto ordered the frame from "Bortolamio, a woodcutter of San Casciano" and asked that it should be "of good, well-seasoned wood," promising in return the sum of eighteen ducats. The following July, Lotto acknowledges his obligations to Durante da Caldarola "who worked for me in Mogliano and set up the altarpiece that I sent from Venice." The composition recalls the *Virgin in Glory with Saints* (plate 180), especially the ecstatic dance of the Saints in the lower half. Behind them the towers and buildings of Rome protrude above the walls. The flaming colors are like Titian's.

Plate 197

THE ASSUMPTION OF THE VIRGIN. *Canvas with molding at the top, 600 × 403. Ancona, Pinacoteca.* Signed and dated 1550. This great canvas was commissioned from Lotto in the will of Lorenzo Tudini (1549) for the Church of San Francesco delle Scale. For it, he was to receive one hundred ducats. On July 1, 1549, the old artist moved to Ancona (he was never to return to Venice) with all his paintings, and was given lodgings in San Francesco where, as he wrote: "I am allowed to work in all privacy." At this point, unfortunately, all inspiration left him. Pallucchini writes: "Lotto's head is unrecognizable. His desire to catch up with the Venice of Titian led him along a false road; the collapse was unavoidable."

Plate 198

THE RETURN OF THE PRODIGAL SON. *Canvas, 50 × 56. Florence, Private Collection.* About 1550-55. Longhi makes the attribution, believing this work to derive from a print by Lucas van Leyden, "an interesting element for whoever attempts to trace the Northern influences in Lotto's mentality" (Boschetto). The attribution is accepted by Coletti who finds in the canvas "evidence that the old painter's inventive power was still fresh and vigorous."

Plate 199

THE ENTOMBMENT. *Canvas, 35 × 55. Florence, Private Collection.* About 1550. Published in *Viatico* by Longhi who dates the execution as above and finds the work "as beautiful as a Renoir of the Cagnes period." In 1946, Locatelli-Milesi published a replica from a private collection at Milan, which Coletti holds is original. A preparatory drawing which may have served for this painting exists in the A. Scharf Collection in London.

Plate 200

MAN WITH AN ARQUEBUS. *Canvas, 94 × 72. Rome, Pinacoteca Capitolina.* About 1551-52. Formerly assigned to Giorgione and attributed to Lotto by Morelli. Coletti dates the portrait 1527-29. Some critics would identify it with the reference in the "Book of Accounts" for 1551-52 to "a portrait of M. Battista, a cross-bowman of Rocca Contrada [now Arcevia]."

Plate 201

THE BAPTISM OF CHRIST. *Canvas, 170 × 135. Loreto, Palazzo Apostolico.* About 1554. This work belongs to the group of paintings done by Lotto for the Choir of the Basilica of Loreto where, as reported by Vasari, "he painted figures as high as an arm or shorter, around the Choir, above the chairs of the priests." Among the works recorded by the biographer are a *Nativity*, an *Adoration of the Magi*, a *Presentation in the Temple*, a *Baptism*, a *Christ and the Adulteress*, *David's Sacrifice* (really a *Sacrifice of Melchizedek*) and a *St Michael*. The assumption may be justified that *The Nativity* (plate 163) and *Christ and the Adulteress* (see comment on plate 142) were painted at an earlier date; the other five have the same height of about one hundred and seventy cms and —with the exception of *The Presentation*, which is unfinished—show signs of work other than Lotto's. Because of the bad condition of these canvases it is impossible to establish who the master's assistants were, though among records of the Santa Casa details have been found of a payment, made on February 6, 1555, to Camillo Bagazzotti di Camerino for "having worked two months and eight days at decorating the Choir with M. Lorenzo Lotto" (Gianuizzi).

Plate 202

THE SACRIFICE OF MELCHIZEDEK. *Canvas, 172 × 248. Loreto, Palazzo Apostolico*. About 1554–56. The composition is almost identical with the one of the same subject in the Bergamo *Intarsias* (plate 90b). The "Book of Accounts" mentions another version: "a great painting with the sacrifice of the King and High Priest Melchizedek when he went to meet Abraham."

Plate 203

THE RECOGNITION OF THE HOLY CHILD. *Canvas, 172 × 255. Loreto, Palazzo Apostolico*. This work is a replica—with variations such as the curtain stretched behind the group—of the Louvre's canvas (plate 163). Most scholars think it was executed about 1535–40, but the dullness of the painting would seem to confirm Berenson's theory that it is not entirely by Lotto. It is wiser, therefore, to place it among Lotto's final works at Loreto.

Plate 204

ST MICHAEL DRIVING LUCIFER OUT OF HEAVEN. *Canvas, 167 × 135. Loreto, Palazzo Apostolico*. About 1554–56. Records show that Lotto had painted an earlier version of this work in March 1542, at Venice: 'an altarpiece with St Michael fighting and expelling Lucifer." Berenson remarks that "contrary to the Renaissance tradition of representing Lucifer as a monster, Lotto shows him as an angel of great beauty."

Plate 205

THE ADORATION OF THE MAGI. *Canvas, 170 × 135. Loreto, Palazzo Apostolico*. Berenson considers this canvas to be inferior in quality to the rest of the series and attributes it to Bagazzotti di Camerino (see comment on plate 201).

Plate 206

THE PRESENTATION IN THE TEMPLE. *Canvas, 170 × 135. Loreto, Palazzo Apostolico*. About 1554–56. Generally considered to be Lotto's last work, this canvas is extraordinarily modern in its power of expression and in its low tonalities of ocher, gray and brown. The figures are sad, spent people, hesitating, as Arcangeli notes, "between infancy and old age." Berenson, who compares it to works by Manet and Degas, calls this composition "perhaps the most modern picture ever painted by an old Italian master." Obviously, the fact that it is unfinished adds to its suggestiveness. (See also plates 207–208.)

Plate 207

THE PRESENTATION IN THE TEMPLE. Detail: Simeon and assistant.

Plate 208

THE PRESENTATION IN THE TEMPLE. Detail: the women at the left.

Plate 209

THE TOILET OF VENUS. *Walnut panel, 177 × 155. Milan, Private Collection*. Dated about 1530. Zampetti, who was the first to publish and illustrate this panel (*Arte Veneta*, 1957, pp. 75–81), relates it to an entry in the "Book of Accounts," for September 1540, in which the artist recorded some expenses he had incurred on behalf of his nephew Mario Carpan "for the adornment of the painting of Venus that I gave him, that is to say the walnut wood, the gilt decoration and the pediment of black canvas of Lyons, with the letters. . . ." The following year Lotto adds that "the painting of Venus is worth approximately thirty ducats." This beautiful panel is so much more precious in that Lotto painted very few female nudes. Against the background of a dark open hall or square, at the right of which are a rose garden, a fountain and some cypresses, the four nudes are represented in languid, elegant poses. A number of Cupids are flying above the group and one of them is placing a crown (or wreath) upon the head of Venus. Zampetti has also published an inscription, which he claims to be in Lotto's hand, on the reverse of the panel. In it the painting is described in terms that are fully consistent with Lotto's written style: "Venus is the symbol of beauty and, assisted by the Graces, she is attending to her toilet: one holds up her mirror, another one arranges her hair and the third one is weaving a golden thread around her head. . . ."

LOST PAINTINGS

A rapid worker, Lotto often went back to his paintings and retouched them, or even, for lack of fresh ideas, copied them altogether. It is not easy to compile a reliable list of his lost works and certainly the hastiness of critics such as Tassi and Locatelli in assigning works by other artists to him has not helped. I have attempted to list here only the works whose existence has been proved by reliable sources, such as the *Cunto de li quadri*, which gives an account of Lotto's activities in Bergamo, and the "Book of Accounts" in which Lotto conscientiously listed his works between 1538 and 1553.

THE RECOGNITION OF THE HOLY CHILD. *Canvas, 125 × 100.* Executed by Lotto about 1537 for Andrea Guzzolini of Osimo. This work remained in the Church of the Minori Osservanti at Osimo until 1866, when it was transferred to the Town Hall in the same city. It was stolen in 1911 and has not been heard of since. Luigi Serra claims that it is now part of a collection in Austria. (See plate 168.)

From the *Cunto de li quadri facti de pictura per mi lorenzo loto a miser Zanin Casoto* (published by Locatelli): "A painting of Christ lying dead in His Mother's arms." "The painting for Zanin's room of a Madonna and Child at the center; on the right is St Julian with the dead father and mother and a small St John the Baptist; on the left is Catrina with the portrait of the above-mentioned Zoannino [*sic*]." "For the room of Misser Juan

Maria: a picture with the Virgin and Child in the center and Juan Maria with his small daughter, Lucretia, on the right; on the left the portrait of his wife and their daughter Isabel (or Elizabeth)."

Adolfo Venturi, who published the "Book of Accounts" drew from it a chronological list of Lotto's works. These are given here, with the exception of works that have been confirmed as still in existence. Works of doubtful identity are included.

1538. Portrait of the Protonotary Gian Maria Pizone (later transformed into a figure of St Bartholomew and presented to the artist's friend, Bartolomeo Carpan). Also for Carpan: a comb-box decorated with grotesques.

1540. A "Venus" for Lotto's nephew, Mario d'Armano, for whom the artist also painted a "Portrait of Martin Luther and his wife," to be presented to a certain Tristan. Also a half-length portrait of Lucretia.

1541. A portrait of Messer Alouise, the son of d'Armano and a portrait of d'Armano's wife. For Ottavio di Macerata: a portrait of his mother, eight drawings of heads (in color); eight landscapes; a sketch of a "Dead Pig with Cherubs" symbolizing luxury; a watercolor of a Nativity; two preparatory drawings of a Tower of Babel; and the Prophet Elijah. A "Picture of Susannah and the Elders" for Mario d'Armano; a "Fainting Virgin"; a portrait of Marcantonio

Giustiniano; a portrait of Marietta Novella, the wife of Tommaso Empoli of Florence; a painting of "Our Lady with a figure on each side," for the tutor of Arman's son.

1542. A picture of "Our Lady with three small Angels" for Lucretia, the daughter of d'Armano, who is about to become a nun; "Our Lady and Christ with small Angels" for Bartolomeo Carpan; a portrait of Liberale da Pinadel; a portrait of Ludovico Avolante; an "Altarpiece with St Michael fighting and expelling Lucifer" for the Provost of San Lio. A "painting for a room of reasonable size, with the Virgin and Christ and St Joseph and the Infant St John the Baptist, with the three Kings" for Mario d'Armano. A portrait of Friar Lorenzo of Bergamo as St Thomas Aquinas. A portrait of Captain Francesco Giustiniani of Treviso; a painted wood Crucifix for Lucretia d'Armano.

1543. A small altarpiece for the main altar of the Church at Breda, with four Angels spreading incense and some Cherubs above them; "a small altarpiece painted in oils with Jesus Christ below and two small Angels" for the townsfolk of Saleto; a portrait of Marcello Framberti of Mantua; two heads of the Redeemer for Friar Sisto in the Church of San Giovanni e Paolo at Venice, painted by Lotto with the assistance of Girolamo da Santacroce.

1544. A St Andrew for Andrea Venier of Treviso; a St Jerome in the Wilderness for Niccolò da Mula; a "large St Jerome and portrait of Donor" for Gironimo Mocenigo; a "head of the Virgin without the Child" for Friar Lorenzo of Bergamo; a gouache of "Our Lord at Prayer in

the Garden" for the Nuns of the Convent of St Clare; a "Madonna of Loreto with SS Sebastian and Rock" for the Friars of Santa Maria Maddalena at Treviso (to which, the following year, Lotto added a figure on either side).

1545. A portrait of Tommaso Costanzo in armor; a new head of the Virgin for Friar Lorenzo of Bergamo; a reproduction of a portrait of Giovanni Aurelio Agurello; a "small picture of Our Lady and Child with SS Zacharias and John" for the gilder, Giovanni Maria. This last work could have been the original of the two replicas in the Poldi-Pezzoli Museum at Milan, and the Basevi Collection at Genoa, described as *Virgin and Child with Zacharias and St John the Baptist* in plate 193.

1546. "The penance of St Mary Magdalen" for Marco Pantia; a portrait of Vincenzo Frigieri, a merchant from Venice; "Our Lady, Jesus Christ, the Saints John the Baptist and Dominic" for Gian Domenico dalla Serena at Murano; a portrait of Matteo Antonino, a Cretan merchant; a portrait of Friar Gregorio of Vicenza, with a Crucifix, the Virgin, the Baptist and the Magdalen; a painting of "Our Lady, the infant St John the Baptist and St Zacharias" for Friar Lorenzo of Pesaro (see the last work listed under 1545).

1547. "Two pictures of Our Lady and sleeping Child" for the gilder Giovanni Maria; a "night scene of a Nativity with Christ shedding light all round" for Gian Domenico dalla Serena; a painting of "the Virgin and Child, two small Angels, SS James and Lawrence" for the Governors of the Mint; a portrait of Giovanni dalla Volta with his wife and two children (Boschetto identifies this work with *Family Group* in the National Gallery, London (plates 71 and 72), but the London work was executed much earlier).

1548. "A life-size painting of Susannah and the Elders both the latter being portraits" for Gian Donato Usper; the portraits of Francesco di Cavali and his wife and children; the portrait of Friar Giovanni Andrea as St Peter Martyr (see plate 195).

1549. "A cover with two small figures showing a fight between Fortitude and Fortune" for a painting which Lotto did not execute but restored for Dario Franceschini of Cingoli; a small painting of the same subject for Rocco, a diamond merchant; a portrait of Girolamo Pulino and his wife (in whose house, in Venice, Lotto stayed as a guest); a St Christopher and nine "small pieces relating the story of the Madonna of Loreto" which Cavalier Philago of Loreto was asked to sell on Lotto's behalf; a portrait of Friar Angelo Ferretti as St Peter Martyr (see last work listed under 1548). A portrait of Pietro Bonarelli of Venice, for whom Lotto also painted "two small pistols lying inside two wicker baskets"; a painting of SS Sebastian and Rock for the Church of San Rocco at Santa Maria Posatora. When this was finished, Lotto replaced a group of women in the background with a St Cyriacus. A second picture of SS Francis and John the Baptist for the same Church; a portrait of Vincenzo Caranzoni, a merchant from Lucca.

1550. Two standards for trumpets for the City of Ancona; a flag with "two figures on each side and other decorations and adornments" for the town of Monte dell'Arno; a small painting of the "Operative Virtue, from which Hope is engendered" for the Venetian diamond merchant, Rocco; a portrait of Alessandro called Robazza as St Alexander in armor; a St Jerome for Giovanni Taurini of Montepulciano.

1551. The portrait of Marin de Poza, a merchant from Ragusa; a portrait of Vincenzo de'Nobili; a St Francis receiving the Stigmata and a St Clare for Francesco Bernabei (who turned down both works). The portrait of Lodovico Grazioli; a portrait of Giovanni Taurini of Montepulciano; three small pictures (SS Elizabeth, Veronica, and the head of St John the Baptist) for Giovanni di Argenta; a portrait of Ercole, a cobbler; a portrait of Abramo, a Portuguese Jew living at Pesaro.

1552. A portrait of Roberto, the son of Vincenzo de'Nobili; a portrait of Vincenzo de'Nobili's major-domo; a portrait (unfinished) of Camillo, a doctor of Macerata; a portrait of Maria, the widow of Antonia Durante dal Monte; a small portrait of Battista, a turner of Venice; twelve Prophets and Sibyls in chiaroscuro; Angels and "Epithets of the Virgin" for the Church of Loreto; a St Francis receiving the Stigmata, a St Jerome and other paintings for the Governor of Loreto. Lotto also painted: the coat of arms of Cardinal di Carpi; two Madonnas of Loreto upon two big candles to be used for Candlemas; ten "little spirits and eight pairs of angel-wings for the Epiphany"; the miracle of the Mayor of Recanati; a Veronica; a Burning Heart with a Crucifix; twenty-six numbered panels for hospital beds; a picture frame; a military flag with an image of the Virgin on both sides.

1552–53. Lotto is asked by Pier Francesco de Amicis to execute a decorated altarpiece for Jesi Cathedral. The price is to be three hundred *scudi*. Lotto signs a contract with Domenico Salimbene who is to provide the glue, wood, metal and the ornaments for the altarpiece; he is assisted in the work by "Antonuzzo, an artist of Jesi." On October 30, 1553, Lotto receives a second payment of one hundred *scudi* "so that we may proceed to gild the ornaments which are at Jesi in the house of Antonuzzo." Of this altarpiece—which must have been Lotto's last great undertaking—no trace remains.

From early sources (Michiel, Ridolfi, Boschini, Campori, Tassi, etc.) as well as from catalogues of sales and collections, it appears that numerous other works by Lotto have been permanently lost. A list of these, derived from a careful and detailed study made by Boschetto, follows:

Bergamo: Church of San Domenico, a fresco with *The Martyrdom of St Catherine*; Church of San Francesco, a fresco with a *Baptism of Christ*; Church of the Trinità, a *Pietà with Saints*; Palazzo del Capitan Grande, *Family Portrait*; Casa Cornello, a *Pietà* and *St Jerome in the Wilderness*; Casa Tassi, *Old Man and Youth with Musical Scores*, a *Madonna with Saints*, a *Marriage of Love*, and a *Nativity*; Casa Gussoni, a *Madonna with Two Saints* and a *Crucifixion*; Casa Pighetti, *Christ Carrying the Cross*; Casa Tassi, a *Dead Christ*; Casa Ragazzoni, *SS Stephen, Rock and Sebastian*; Casa Bettame, *Female Bust* and *St Jerome in the Wilderness*; Casa Morandi, *Portrait of*

Donna Laura; Casa Casotti, *The Flight into Egypt*; Casa Albani, *Portrait of F. Albani*; Casa Zanchi, *Nativity* (with a portrait of D. Tassi); Picinelli Collection, *Four Saints*; Frizzoni Collection, *Two Angels* (fragment of fresco).

London: Yarborough Collection, *Portrait of a Man*.

Milan: Archbishopric, *Recognition of the Child*.

Parma: Palazzo del Giardino, *Double Portrait*.

Pat (North Italy): Manzoni Collection, *Portrait of a Man* and *Entombment with Fainting Virgin*.

Ranica (Bergamo): Parish Church, *Christ and the Apostles*.

Rome: Church of the Gesù, *Sacred History*; Palazzo Accoramboni, *The Presentation in the Temple, SS Sebastian and Francis* and a *Calvary*; Spiridon Collection, *Portrait* (signed and dated 1531).

Treviso: Riformati, *Madonna and Child*; Casa Collalta, *Portrait of "One of the Family"*; Casa Unigo, *Portrait of a Priest*.

Venice: Giovanelli Collection, *St Nicholas*; Renieri Collection, *The Road to Calvary*; Savorgnan Collection, *Portrait of an Old Man*; Sernagiotto-Cerato Collection, various paintings; Spietra Collection, *St Jerome in the Wilderness*, a *Madonna* and a *Portrait*.

Wentworth Castle: *Portrait of a Man*.

Unknown location: *St Jerome in the Wilderness* (mentioned by Campori from a seventeenth-century catalogue).

PAINTINGS
ATTRIBUTED TO LOTTO

Plate 210

PORTRAIT OF A MAN WEARING A RED CAP. *Venice, Museo Correr*. The attribution is by Coletti (1939). Longhi supports Crowe and Caval-caselle in assigning it to Carpaccio and rejecting the vague attribution to the School of Ferrara. Exhibited at Venice in 1953.

Plate 211

PORTRAIT OF A YOUTH. *Bergamo, Accademia Carrara*. Originally attributed to Holbein and Jacopo de' Barbari and later assigned to Lotto by Frizzoni. Boschetto dates it about 1500. The style in this portrait which seems to have been engraved rather than painted, leads us to doubt Lotto's authorship. It was, however, shown at the Venice Exhibition.

Plates 212–13

HERALDS ON THE ONIGO MONU-MENT. *Treviso, Church of San Niccolò. Detached frescoes transferred to canvas*. Traditionally attributed to Antonello da Messina, Giovanni Bellini and Jacopo de' Barbari. Assigned to Lotto by Biscaro, supported by Coletti, who sees in these figures further evidence that Lotto was pictorially educated in the Marches. The inspiration for these heralds, however, could equally have come from Milan. Fiocco and Longhi refer directly to a Bramante in the Casa Panigarola and to Bonconsiglio. The controversial date of execution is set between 1498 and 1506. These monu-mental heralds, portrayed with great assurance, seem to reveal the hand of an expert craftsman rather than that of a beginner such as Lotto must have been in the last years of the fifteenth century. This fresco decoration was exhibited with Lotto's other works at Venice in 1953.

Plate 214

DEAD CHRIST IN LANDSCAPE. *Asolo, Parish Church*. In Longhi's opinion, these are the top and predella of *The Assumption* (see comment on plate 7). Exhibited at Venice in 1953.

Plate 215

SKETCHES FROM THE LEGEND OF ST STEPHEN. *Bergamo, Accademia Carrara*. These sketches for a pre-della were attributed to Schiavone until Morelli assigned them to Lotto with general agreement. Berenson calls them as "modern as Delacroix." Pallucchini, however, favors the authorship of Marescalco, and Bosch-etto ascribes the sketches to an "out-of-date provincial" of about the end of the sixteenth century.

Plate 216

CHRIST LEAVING THE HALL OF JUDGMENT. *Milan, Private Collection*. The attribution is by Longhi and the execution is dated about 1524. There is, however, a large discrepancy between the orderly universe of this magnificent canvas (governed with geometrical clarity in the distribution of tones and in the perspective) and Lotto's sentimental world. An artist under the later influence of Bramantino seems more likely. Exhibited at Venice in 1953.

MADONNA AND CHILD WITH WORSHIPPER. *Basel, Kunstmuseum.* Attributed to Lotto by Longhi and dated about 1500. Coletti assigns it to P. M. Pennacchi. Exhibited at Venice in 1953.

ST CATHERINE OF ALEXANDRIA. *Milan, Poldi-Pezzoli Museum.* A small panel, probably a replica of the original Kress masterpiece (plate 62). Exhibited at Venice in 1953.

VIRGIN AND CHILD WITH ZACHARIAS AND ST JOHN THE BAPTIST. *Genoa, Basevi Collection.* Attributed to Lotto by Longhi Probably a replica of the Poldi-Pezzoli canvas (plate 193). Exhibited at Venice in 1953.

ASSASSINATION OF ST PETER MARTYR. *Alzano, Parish Church.* The attribution to Lotto was rejected by Longhi (1926) who assigned the work to Palma Vecchio. Berenson, on the other hand, defended it vigorously at the time, though later (1955) admitted that some parts may be the work of Palma Vecchio. But he insisted that the conception and the greater part of the execution are by Lotto, influenced by Palma Vecchio.

NUDE VENUS IN LANDSCAPE. *Bergamo, Private Collection.* The attribution is by Longhi who dates the painting about 1503. Berenson accepted this in 1955, and said that the picture is now in a private collection at Milan.

MADONNA AND SAINTS. *Milan, Archbishopric.* Old copy.

PORTRAIT OF A GENTLEMAN. *Formerly in London, Duveen Collection.* The attribution is by Coletti. Assigned to Giovanni Bellini by Berenson, Longhi and others.

PIETÀ. *Frankfurt-am-Main, Hartmann Collection.* The attribution is by Dussler and Coletti.

BUST OF A YOUTH AGAINST A GREEN CURTAIN. *Vienna, Kunsthistorisches Museum.* Signed, but Boschetto thinks that the signature is false and Berenson (1955) stated that, but for the signature, "one scarcely would have dared to ascribe this masterpiece to Lotto."

BUST OF A YOUNG MAN. *Ascott, National Trust.* Assigned to Lotto in the Ascott catalogue and by Berenson. Exhibited at Venice in 1953.

ST JEROME IN HIS STUDY. *Rome, Zocca Collection.* Attributed to Lotto by Coletti and Berenson. Derived from the well-known Dürer etching of 1514.

MADONNA AND SAINTS. *Settignano, Berenson Collection.* The original attribution by the owner was accepted by Coletti, but later (1955) Berenson himself expressed doubts.

PORTRAIT OF CARDINAL POMPEO COLONNA. *Rome, Colonna Gallery.* The attribution is by Venturi. Berenson at first described it as an "almost contemporary copy," but later (1955) accepted Lotto's authorship.

HEAD OF A WOMAN. *Bergamo, Count Secco Suardo Collection.* The attribution is by V. Bernardi. Berenson does not reject it but expresses doubts.

VIRGIN AND CHILD WITH ST FRANCIS. *Budapest, Museum of Fine Arts.* The attribution is by Venturi. Longhi and Berenson ascribe it to a follower of Lotto.

PORTRAIT OF THE PROTONOTARY, GIOVANNI GIULIANO. *London, National Gallery.* Assigned to Lotto by Berenson and Venturi, and to Moretto by Longhi.

PORTRAIT OF A WOMAN. *Leningrad, Hermitage.* Attributed to Lotto by Venturi and to Moretto by Longhi.

ST JEROME IN THE WILDERNESS. *Hamburg, Kunsthalle.* Accepted as a work by Lotto by Venturi, Biagi, Coletti, and Berenson. Longhi assigns it to an exponent of the School of Ferrara. Exhibited at Venice in 1953.

THE MARRIAGE OF THE VIRGIN. *Formerly at Milan, Private Collection.* Attributed to Lotto by Longhi. Coletti claims that it is signed. Berenson rejects the attribution.

NARCISSUS AT THE POOL. *Rome, Meyer Collection.* Attributed to Lotto by Venturi.

ST SEBASTIAN. *Bologna, Private Collection.* The attribution is by Longhi. A replica of the *St Sebastian* at Berlin (plate 152a).

PORTRAIT OF A GENTLEMAN. *Stockholm, Museum.* The attribution is by Sirén. Berenson accepts it, Boschetto and Coletti reject it. Exhibited at Venice in 1953.

PORTRAIT OF MICHELANGELO (?). *Nancy, Museum.* Attributed to Lotto by Berenson and to Brusasorci by Longhi. Exhibited at Venice in 1953.

SS CATHERINE AND GEMINIAN. *Venice, Church of San Marco. Mosaics.* The attribution, by Muraro, is rejected by Berenson.

BUST OF A BEARDED YOUNG MAN. *Hampton Court, Royal Gallery.* Doubtfully attributed to Lotto by Crowe and Cavalcaselle. Berenson is sure that the work is by Lotto. Longhi rejects the attribution.

BUST OF A MAN. *Hampton Court, Royal Gallery.* An inscription in the picture reads: CARPENDO CARPERIS IPSE. The attribution to Lotto by Coletti is rejected by Boschetto who writes: "The work does not even look Italian." Berenson, who at first shared Coletti's views, later (1955) changed his mind.

BUST OF A YOUTH. *Hampton Court, Royal Gallery.* Traditionally assigned to Dosso, the picture is attributed to Lotto by Coletti and Berenson.

PORTRAIT OF A YOUNG MAN IN A NICHE. *Bordeaux, Museum.* The attribution is by Berenson and Coletti. Longhi assigns it to Palma. Exhibited at Venice in 1953.

PORTRAIT OF A GENTLEMAN WITH A SMALL BOOK. *Vicenza, Museum.* Berenson (with doubts) and Coletti attribute this panel transferred to canvas to Lotto. Boschetto is waiting for the picture to be restored before submitting an opinion.

PORTRAIT OF A MAN. *Los Angeles, Museum.* The attribution is by Coletti. Boschetto describes it as "a Northern work."

PORTRAIT OF A PRELATE. *Rome, Albertini Collection.* The attribution is by Coletti and Berenson. Longhi thinks that this painting came originally from the region of Friuli (in the Venezia Giulia).

MALE PORTRAIT. *Munich, Fleischmann Collection.* Attributed to Lotto by Coletti and Berenson.

PORTRAIT OF A MAN. *New York, Metropolitan Museum of Art.* The attribution is by Berenson and Coletti.

PORTRAIT OF A YOUNG MAN. *New York, Metropolitan Museum of Art.* Attributed to Lotto by Coletti and to Savoldo by Berenson.

ST SEBASTIAN. *Formerly at Dresden.* The attribution is by Loeser and Coletti. Berenson assigns it to an imitator and Longhi to Annibale Carracci.

PORTRAIT OF A WOMAN. *Amsterdam, Rijksmuseum.* Attributed to Lotto by Coletti and catalogued by the Museum as of the Florentine School.

PORTRAIT OF A WARRIOR. *Amsterdam, Rijksmuseum.* Catalogued as a work by Lotto. Longhi calls it a copy of a work by Titian.

PORTRAIT OF A MAN. *New York, Wildenstein Collection.* Signed and dated 1541. The attribution, by Biagi, is accepted by Berenson. Boschetto is doubtful about both signature and date.

PORTRAIT OF A MAN. *Budapest, Museum of Fine Arts.* Attributed to Lotto by A. Venturi and Biagi. Generally asigned to Moretto.

PORTRAIT OF A GENTLEMAN. *Cassel, Museum.* Berenson assigns it to Lotto, and Longhi to an unknown artist from Brescia.

NESSUS AND DEIANIRA. *Amsterdam, Lanz Collection.* The attribution, by Schubring, is rejected by Boschetto who assigns it to "the circle of Schiavone."

PORTRAIT OF A MAN. Formerly in Berlin and part of the Coray Sale, when it was catalogued as a work by Lotto.

PORTRAIT OF A MAN IN HIS STUDY. *Brescia, Palazzo Martinengo Salvadego.* The attribution is by Moschini, but Crowe and Cavalcaselle and Longhi assign it to Moretto. Berenson admits that it looks "very Morettesque."

PORTRAIT. *Darmstadt, Museum.* Attributed to Lotto by Crowe and Cavalcaselle; Longhi and Boschetto believe it may be by Palma.

PORTRAIT OF A MAN. *Detroit, Museum of Fine Art.* Berenson thinks it "hazardous to make a definite attribution" and Longhi believes it to have been painted in Parma.

PORTRAIT OF A YOUTH. *Dublin, National Gallery of Ireland.* Doubtfully ascribed to Lotto by Berenson. Longhi assigns it to "Paris / Licinio."

PORTRAIT. *Hereford, Eastnor Castle, Lord Somers' Collection.* The attribution, by A. Venturi, is rejected by Boschetto.

NATIVITY BY NIGHT. *Florence, Uffizi.* Previously in the Ferroni Collection. Attributed to Lotto by Frizzoni and Berenson. Longhi and Coletti believe it to be a copy. The picture repeats the principal scenes of the Siena *Nativity* (plate 120).

SEATED GENTLEMAN (also known as SEBASTIAN CABOT). *Harewood*

House (*Yorks.*), *Earl of Harewood Collection*. Longhi believes it is "provincial Venetian."

PORTRAIT. *London, Ruck Collection*. Attributed to Lotto by R. Fry. Boschetto remarks that it does not look Italian.

PORTRAIT OF A MONK. *Rush H. Kress Collection, New York*. The attribution is by Berenson. Longhi believes it to have come from Lombardy.

TWO LADIES. *Milan, Castello Sforzesco*. The attribution is by Berenson. Longhi sees in it the hand of the seventeenth-century imitator of Lotto, Liberi.

LOT AND HIS DAUGHTERS. *Milan, Castello Sforzesco*. The attribution by Morelli is rejected by Berenson who assigns it to Cariani.

SO-CALLED PORTRAIT OF HENRY VIII. *Naples, Royal Palace*. The attribution is by Berenson. Others believe it the work of Parmigianino and Longhi called it a "Northern work."

PORTRAIT OF A YOUNG PRELATE DRESSED IN WHITE. *Naples, Pinacoteca*. Attributed by Berenson to Lotto, by Suida to Luini, and by Boschetto to a Lombard-Emilian artist.

PORTRAIT OF A MAN WITH A SKULL. *Location unknown*. Berenson admits that this portrait, "so very Lottesque, leaves me a trifle perplexed rather than doubtful." Mather assigns it to Lotto but Boschetto describes it as from the provinces, Friuli probably.

PORTRAIT OF A WOMAN AS ST URSULA. *New York, Aran Collection*.

The attribution is by Venturi. Boschetto rejects it on chronological grounds and further: "it is perhaps not even Venetian."

PORTRAIT OF GIULIO MELLINI. *Paris, Louvre*. Attributed to Lotto by Venturi and by Boschetto to "perhaps Catena."

THE REDEEMER. *Formerly Richmond (Surrey), Cook Collection*. The attribution is by Venturi. Others believe it the work of Jacopo de'Barbari, and Berenson assigns it to Cima da Conegliano.

SACRA CONVERSAZIONE. *Rome, Borghese Gallery*. For Berenson this is a copy of a lost Lotto. Other critics are doubtful. Longhi thinks that it may be an early Palma.

PORTRAIT OF A SCHOLAR. *Rovigo, Accademia dei Concordi*. Attributed to Lotto by Venturi.

PORTRAIT OF A MAN WITH A FOLDED LETTER IN HIS HAND. *Venice, Galleria dell'Accademia*. The attribution, by Fogolari, is accepted by Berenson. Boschetto does not reject it but is not entirely satisfied that it is by Lotto.

AN ANGEL APPEARING TO ST ROCK. *Formerly Venice, Giovanelli Collection*. Attributed to Lotto by Crowe and Cavalcaselle and "in part, at least" by Berenson. Boschetto describes it as a "Bergamesque work."

MADONNA WITH SAINTS AND DONOR. *Vercelli, Museo Borgogna*. Attributed to Lotto by Crowe and Cavalcaselle and to Palma by Boschetto.

PORTRAIT OF A YOUTH. *Formerly Vienna, Figdor Collection.* The attribution is by Baldass. Boschetto describes it as "reflecting the Friuli atmosphere."

ST JEROME IN THE WILDERNESS. *Sinaia, Castle of Peles.* The attribution by Busuioceanu, is accepted by Berenson.

PORTRAIT OF A LADY. *Formerly London, Holford Collection.* Catalogued as a Lotto in this Collection. Berenson and Fiocco reject the attribution.

PORTRAIT OF A MAN. *London, Rothermere Collection.* Catalogued as a Lotto, but Longhi and Boschetto describe it as a "Northern work."

PORTRAIT OF THE POET, MELDOLLA. *Formerly Milan, Agosti Mendoza Collection.* The attribution is traditional. Longhi however, believes it to be a work painted in Brescia.

ST STEPHEN. *Munich, Messinger Collection.* Catalogued as a Lotto, but Boschetto rejects the attribution.

THE MARRIAGE OE ST CATHERINE. *Formerly Munich, Rohoncz Collection.* Attributed to Lotto by Van Marle. Longhi believes it to be an imitation of Pietro Vecchia by Romanino.

PORTRAIT OF A BEARDED MAN. *Formerly Munich, Rohoncz Collection.* The attribution to Lotto, by Gronau, Hadeln and Mayer, is accepted by Van Marle. Boschetto states that if this is the same portrait which later reappeared in the Metropolitan Museum of Art at New York, then the attribution should be rejected.

PORTRAIT OF A PHYSICIAN. *Formerly in New York and part of the Padini Sale.* Catalogued as a work by Lotto, but he is emphatically not the painter.

JUDITH. *Formerly in Paris, Sedelmayer Sale.* The attribution, made in the catalogue of the Sale, is rejected by Venturi.

PORTRAIT OF A LADY. *Formerly in Paris, Sedelmayer Sale.* Attributed to Lotto in the catalogue, but Boschetto believes it to be the work of an artist from Brescia, datable in the first half of the sixteenth century.

MADONNA AND CHILD WITH THE INFANT ST JOHN THE BAPTIST. *Formerly Quinto di Sesto Fiorentino Purves Carter Collection.* Catalogued as a Lotto, but it is in fact a copy of a work by Palma.

MADONNA AND CHILD WITH SAINTS AND DONOR. *Formerly Quinto di Sesto Fiorentino, Purves Carter Collection.* Attributed to Lotto in the catalogue, but it is by Jacopo Bassano or one of his followers.

PORTRAIT OF A YOUTH. *Rome, Galleria Nazionale.* Berenson, who thought it a copy, accepted the attribution to Lotto after the picture was cleaned and restored.

ST JEROME IN THE WILDERNESS. *Rome, Scarpitti Collection.* The attribution is by Venturi. Boschetto considers it a work executed in the seventeenth century.

ST DOMINIC. *Rome, Scarpitti Collection.* The attribution is by Venturi.

CHRIST RESURRECTED. *Rovetta con Fino (Bergamo), Church of Ognissanti.* The attribution to Lotto, in the Church inventory, is rejected by Boschetto.

CRUCIFIXION. *Stuttgart, Museum.* Attributed to Lotto in the catalogue.

NATIVITY WITH DONOR. *Venice, Accademia.* Berenson, in listing this canvas with Lotto's works, admits "I believe it to have been painted by Moretto, who elsewhere shows signs of having been influenced by Lotto."

PORTRAIT OF A WOMAN. *Worcester, Massachusetts.* Catalogue attribution. This work, however, is too remote from Lotto.

CHRIST AND THE ADULTERESS. *Genoa, Galleria Durazzo Adorno.* Catalogued as a work by Lotto.

PORTRAIT OF A GENTLEMAN. *Bergamo, Cugini Collection.* Published in *Galetti e Camesasca.* The attribution is by Venturi. Coletti reads in the dedication the name, Giberto I da Correggio.

PORTRAIT OF A MAN WITH GLOVES. *Birmingham, Alabama, Museum of Art (S. H. Kress Collection).* Attributed in the catalogue.

MADONNA AND CHILD WITH SS JAMES AND LUCY. *Vienna, Private Collection.* Published by Otto Benesch (in *Studies in the History of Art, dedicated to W. E. Suida*, 1959, pp. 240–43), who claims that the panel came from Bergamo. Benesch assigns it to Lotto's late period and relates it to *The Presentation in the Temple* at Loreto. But a certain mannerism in the execution of the two rather static, elongated figures at the sides, and the figure of the Child, leaves one in some doubt as to the validity of this attribution.

The great exhibition of Lotto's works held at Venice in the summer of 1953, and more especially the two comprehensive publications by Luigi

Colletti and Bernard Berenson (see Bibliographical Note), have produced numerous attributions in addition to those already listed in this work. This is particularly true of portraits assigned to Lotto; on the other hand, Berenson who submitted a great number of these attributions in 1955, carefully points how difficult it is to be sure, especially when establishing the authorship of portraits.

We therefore think it necessary to list below the works, not mentioned before, attributed to Lotto by Coletti and Berenson.

Attributions by
LUIGI COLETTI:

Portrait of a Man, Philadelphia, Johnson Collection; *Two Saints*, Venice, Private Collection; *St Francis*, Genoa, Nigro Collection; *Portrait of a Youth*, Switzerland, Private Collection; *Portrait of a Man* (Correggio's *Doctor*), Dresden, Gemäldegalerie; *Natvity*, Venice, Private Collection; *Portrait of a Woman*, Switzerland, Private Collection; *Portrait of Count Acqua*, Milan, Private Collection; *Portrait of a Man with Pendant*, Venice, Cini Collection; *Portrait of a Bearded Prelate*, Texas, Houston Museum; *Portrait of a Man*, Venice, Private Collection; *Votive Offering*, Venice, Private Collection; *Ecce Homo* and *The Crowning with Thorns*, Venice, Private Collection; *Landscape*, California, San Diego Museum; *Portrait of a Man*, Oderzo, Vizzotto Collection; *The Entombment*, Milan, Private Collection.

Attributions by
BERNARD BERENSON:

Bust of Man, Vienna, Kunsthistorisches Museum (*c.* 1505); *Bust of a Young Prelate*, formerly Paris, Heugel Collection; *Portrait of a Young Cardinal*, New York, Mogmar Foundation; *Young man with a Small Book*, formerly Vienna, Private Collection; *Portrait of Francesco Soderini*, formerly Kinnel, Hughes Collection; *Doctor Leoniceno*, formerly Milan, Crespi Collection; *Head of a Bearded Man*, formerly London, Miss Mundella Collection; *Portrait of a Dignitary*, formerly Westport, Sligo Collection; *Portrait of Antonio Correr*, formerly London, Ricketts, and Shannon; *Portrait of Laura Pisani*, Cornbury Park, Watney Collection; *Portrait Bust of a Man Aged Thirty-One*, formerly Amsterdam, Goudstikker Collection; *Portrait of a Gentleman*, New York, Mortimer Brandt Collection; *Portrait of Andrea Navagero*, Eastnor Castle, Bathurst Collection; *Portrait of a Man in His Study*, formerly Parkenkirchen, Wigger Collection; *Portrait of a Man in a Fur Coat* (doubtful), Stuttgart, Museum; *Portrait of a Seated Gentleman* (doubtful), formerly Ashridge Park, Brownlow Collection; *Portrait of a Sculptor*, Mexico City, F. Mayer Collection; *Portrait* (miniature), Paris, Private Collection; *Man with a Skull*, *Portrait of a Lady* (doubtful), *Nativity* (lunette), and *A Gentleman*, formerly Rome, Paolini Collection; *Bust of a Man* (doubtful), and *Man in a Fur Coat*, Copenhagen, Museum; *Portrait of a Gentleman*, Paris, Sachs Collection; *Head of St John the Baptist on a Plate*, Cleveland, Museum of Art; *Portrait of a Venetian Councillor* (doubtful), St Louis, Museum; *Portrait of Giovanni Cornaro* (doubtful), Althrop (Northampton), Lord Spencer Collection; *Bust of a Man* (doubtful), formerly Beachhurst (N.Y.), Loevenich Collection; *Portrait of a Bearded Scholar*, Southampton (N.Y.), Museum; *Portrait of a Young Woman* (doubtful), formerly Paris, Maitland Collection; *Portrait of an Astronomer*, formerly New York, Van Dieman Galleries; *Bust of a Man in Profile*, Switzerland, Private Collection; *Bust of a Man*, Milan, Vernier Collection; *Portrait of a Friar* (1546), homeless; *Portrait of a Man*, formerly Vienna, Offenheim Collection; *Portrait of a Scribe*, New York, F. Martin Joseph Collection; *Portrait of an Aged Scholar*, Tunis, V. Guez Collection; *Portrait of a Man with His Hand in His Belt*, New York, A. Platt Collection; *Allegory of Venus and Cupid*, Paris, Louvre (Grasset Bequest); *Portrait of an Aged Prelate*, Rheims, Museum; *Portrait of an Old Man with a Gray Beard*, Washington, D.C., Johnson Collection; *Octagonal Ceiling with Allegory of the Arts of the Quadrivium*, Florence, Van Hadeln Collection.

LOCATION OF PAINTINGS

ALLENTOWN (PENNSYLVANIA)

MUSEUM OF ART (S. H. Kress Collection)
St Jerome Penitent (plate 32b).

ANCONA

PINACOTECA
The Assumption of the Virgin (plate 197).
SANTA MARIA DELLA PIAZZA
Madonna Enthroned with Four Saints (plate 174).

ASOLO

PARISH CHURCH
The Assumption of the Virgin (plates 7–8).
Dead Christ in Landscape (plate 214; attribution).

BANBURY (OXFORDSHIRE)

UPTON HOUSE
Bust of a Dominican Monk (plate 18).

BERGAMO

ACCADEMIA CARRARA
The Martyrdom of St Stephen (plates 38, 41–42).
The Deposition (plate 39).
The Miracle of St Dominic (plate 40).
Portrait of Lucina Brembate (plate 53).
The Marriage of St Catherine (plates 64–66).
Holy Family with St Catherine (plate 161).
Portrait of a Youth (plate 211; attribution).

Sketches from the Legend of St Stephen (plate 215; attribution).
CHURCH OF SAN BARTOLOMEO
Madonna Enthroned with Saints (plates 36–37).
CHURCH OF SAN BERNARDINO IN PIGNOLO
The San Bernardino Altarpiece (plates 50–52).
CHURCH OF SAN MICHELE AL POZZO BIANCO
God the Father Supported by Angels (plate 98).
The Annunciation (plates 99a and b).
The Birth of the Virgin (plates 100, 102).
The Presentation in the Temple and *The Marriage of the Virgin* (plate 101).
The Visitation (plate 103).
CHURCH OF SANT'ALESSANDRO DELLA CROCE
Holy Trinity (plate 49a).
CHURCH OF SANT'ALESSANDRO IN COLONNA
The Deposition (plate 47).
CHURCH OF SANTA MARIA MAGGIORE
Intarsias (plates 88–93).
CHURCH OF SANTO SPIRITO
The Santo Spirito Altarpiece (plates 54–55).

BERLIN

STAATLICHES MUSEEN
Christ Taking Leave of His Mother (plates 56–58).
Portrait of an Architect (plate 105).

Portrait of a Youth Against a Green Curtain (plate 106).
Bust of a Youth Against a Red Curtain (plate 114).
St Sebastian (plate 152a).
St Christopher (plate 152b).

LEPKE COLLECTION (formerly)
Double Portrait (plate 70).

BIRMINGHAM (ALABAMA)

MUSEUM OF ART (S. H. Kress Collection)
Portrait of a Man with Gloves (attribution).

Boston PR.60

BRESCIA

PINACOTECA TOSIO-MARTINENGO
The Adoration of the Shepherds (plates 129–130).

BUDAPEST

MUSEUM OF FINE ARTS
Angel with Globe and Scepter (plate 43a).
Apollo Asleep on Parnassus (plate 143).

CAMBRIDGE (MASSACHUSETTS)

FOGG ART MUSEUM
Portrait of a Dominican Friar as St Peter Martyr (plate 195).

CELANA (BERGAMO)

CHURCH OF SANTA MARIA ASSUNTA
The Assumption of the Virgin (plate 115).

CHICAGO (ILLINOIS)

J. W. ELLSWORTH COLLECTION (formerly)
Portrait of Christopher Columbus (plate 34b).

CINGOLI (MACERATA)

CHURCH OF SAN DOMENICO
The Madonna of the Rosary (plates 169–173).

CLEVELAND (OHIO)

MUSEUM OF ART
Man on a Terrace (plate 121).

COSTA DI MEZZATE (BERGAMO)

CAMOZZI COLLECTION
Madonna and Child with Two Saints (plate 61).

CREDARO (BERGAMO)

CHURCH OF SAN GIORGIO
God the Father (plate 94a).
St George Slaying the Dragon (plate 94b).
The Nativity with SS Rock and Sebastian (plate 95).
SS Jerome and Anthony of Padua (?) (plate 96a).
St Lawrence (plate 96b).
SS Bartholomew and Catherine of Alexandria (plate 97a).
St George (plate 97b).

DIJON

MUSEUM
Bust of a Woman (plate 6).

DRESDEN (formerly)

GEMÄLDEGALERIE
Madonna and Child with the Infant St John (plate 48b).

EDINBURGH

NATIONAL GALLERY OF SCOTLAND
Sacra Conversazione (plate 1b).

EL PASO (TEXAS)

MUSEUM OF ART (S. H. Kress Collection)

Portrait of a Man with Symbols
(plate 185).

FLORENCE

BERENSON COLLECTION
Christ on the Cross with the Symbols of the Passion (plate 147).

CONTINI-BONACOSSI COLLECTION
Susannah and the Elders (plates 45–46).
Madonna and Child with Saints (plate 59).

R. LONGHI COLLECTION
St Peter Martyr (plate 43b).
A Dominican Saint (plate 43c).

PRIVATE COLLECTIONS
The Return of the Prodigal Son (plate 198).
The Entombment (plate 199).

UFFIZI
Portrait of a Youth (plate 2).
Virgin and Child with SS Anne, Joachim and Jerome (plate 162).

GIOVINAZZO (BARI)

CHURCH OF SAN DOMENICO
St Felix (plate 181).

HAMPTON COURT

ROYAL GALLERY
Portrait of Andrea Odoni (plates 123–24).

JESI

PINACOTECA
The Deposition (plate 28).
SS Francis and Clare (plate 107a).
Madonna Enthroned with Saints (plate 107b).
The Archangel Gabriel and *The Annunciate Virgin* (plates 108–09).
The Annunciation, lunette (plate 145a).

The Visitation (plates 145b, 146).
The St Lucy Altarpiece (plates 154–55).
Scenes from the Legend of St Lucy (plates 156–59).

KRAKOW (formerly)

PUSLOWSKI COLLECTION
Sacra Conversazione (plate 26b).

LENINGRAD

HERMITAGE
Christ Leading the Apostles to Mount Tabor (plate 30).
Virgin Nursing the Christ Child (plate 48a).

LONDON

BENSON COLLECTION (formerly)
Dead Christ Supported by Two Angels (plate 33a).

DUKE OF NORTHUMBERLAND COLLECTION
Cherub with a Skull (plate 49b).

NATIONAL GALLERY
Portrait of Agostino and Niccolo Della Torre (plate 35b).
Madonna and Child with Saints (plate 60). Boston
Family Group (plates 71–72).
Portrait of a Lady as Lucretia (plate 136).

DOETSCH COLLECTION (formerly)
Portrait of Piero Soderini (plate 34a).

LORETO

PALAZZO APOSTOLICO
SS Rock, Christopher, and Sebastian (plate 153).
The Baptism of Christ (plate 201).
The Sacrifice of Melchizedek (plate 202).
The Recognition of the Holy Child (plate 203).
St Michael Driving Lucifer out of Heaven (plate 204).

The *Adoration of the Magi* (plate 205).
The *Presentation in the Temple* (plates 206–08).

MADRID

PRADO
Portrait of Messer Marsilio and His Bride (plate 69).
St Jerome in the Wilderness (plate 190).

MILAN

BRERA GALLERY
The Assumption of the Virgin (plate 31).
Portrait of Messer Febo da Brescia (plate 182).
Portrait of Laura da Pola (plate 183).
Portrait of an Old Man (plate 184).
Portrait of an Elderly Gentleman (plate 186).
Pietà (plate 189).

CASTELLO SFORZESCO
Portrait of a Young Man (plate 110).

CRESPI COLLECTION
Male Portrait (plate 144).

PRIVATE COLLECTIONS
The Toilet of Venus (plate 209).
Christ Leaving the Hall of Judgment (plate 216; attribution).

POLDI-PEZZOLI MUSEUM
Madonna and Child with Zacharias and St John the Baptist (plate 193).

MOGLIANO (MACERATA)

PARISH CHURCH
Madonna in Glory with Saints (plate 196).

MONTE SAN GIUSTO (MACERATA)

CHURCH OF SANTA MARIA IN TELUSIANO
The Crucifixion (plates 148–151).

MUNICH

ALTE PINAKOTHEK
The Marriage of St Catherine (plates 9a and b).

NAPLES

PINACOTECA NAZIONALE
Madonna and Child with Saints (plate 1a).
Portrait of Bishop Bernardo de' Rossi (plate 3).

NEW ORLEANS (LOUSIANA)

DELGADO MUSEUM OF ART (S. H. Kress Collection)
Portrait of a Gentleman (plate 160).

NEW YORK

HEARST COLLECTION (formerly)
Madonna in Landscape with Two Donors (plate 113).

NIVAAGAARD (COPENHAGEN)

HAGE COLLECTION
Portrait of a Man with a Rosary (plate 33b).

OSIMO

TOWN HALL (formerly)
The Recognition of the Holy Child (plate 168).

OXFORD

CHRIST CHURCH LIBRARY
Christ at Emmaus (plate 192).

PARIS

LOUVRE
St Jerome in the Wilderness (plate 10).
Christ and the Adulteress (plate 142).
The Recognition of the Holy Child (plate 163).

PHILADELPHIA

J. G. JOHNSON COLLECTION
Madonna and Child with Four Saints
(plate 44).
Portrait of the Surgeon Stuer with His Son (plate 188).

PONTERANICA (BERGAMO)

CHURCH OF SANTI VINCENZO ED ALESSANDRO
The Ponteranica Polyptych (plates 116–19).

PRINCETON (NEW JERSEY)

UNIVERSITY MUSEUM
Holy Family with St Gabriel (plate 26a).

RALEIGH (NORTH CAROLINA)

MUSEUM OF ART (S. H. Kress Collection)
Martyrdom of St Alexander (plate 43d).
Dead Christ Supported by Angels (plate 43e).

RECANATI

PINACOTECA
The Recanati Polyptych (plates 19–23, 24a and b).
The Transfiguration (plate 29).

CHURCH OF SAN DOMENICO
St Vincent Ferrer in Glory (plate 27a).

CHURCH OF SANTA MARIA SOPRA MERCANTI
St James the Pilgrim (plate 27b).
The Annunciation (plate 132).

ROME

CASTEL SANT'ANGELO
St Jerome in the Wilderness (plate 11).

BORGHESE GALLERY
Madonna and Child with Saints (plate 17).
Portrait of a Gentleman Dressed in Black (plates 139–141).

DORIA GALLERY
Portrait of a Man Aged Thirty-Seven (plate 166).
St Jerome in the Wilderness (plate 179).

GALLERIA NAZIONALE
The Marriage of St Catherine (plates 67–68).

PINACOTECA CAPITOLINA
Man with an Arquebus (plate 200).

ROSPIGLIOSI-PALLAVICINI COLLECTION
The Allegory of Chastity (plates 137–38).

SANTA MONICA (CALIFORNIA)

PAUL J. GETTY COLLECTION
Portrait of a Jeweler (plate 35a).

SARASOTA (FLORIDA)

THE RINGLING MUSEUM OF ART
Madonna with Sleeping Child (plate 165).

SEDRINA (BERGAMO)

PARISH CHURCH
Madonna in Glory with Saints (plate 180).

SIBIU (RUMANIA)

BRUCKENTHAL GALLERY
St Jerome in the Wilderness (plate 23a).

SIENA

PINACOTECA
The Nativity (plate 120).

SPLIT (YUGOSLAVIA)

MONASTERO DELLE PALUDI
Portrait of Bishop Tommaso Negri
(plate 122).

TRESCORE (BERGAMO)

SUARDI CHAPEL
The Legend of St Barbara (plates 73–79, folding reproduction).
St Clare Taking Her Vows (plates 80–81).
Miracles of St Clare (plates 82–84).
The Beheading of St Catherine of Alexandria (plate 85a).
The Communion of Mary Magdalen (plate 85b).
The Erythraean Sibyl (plate 86a).
The Prophet Isaiah (plate 86b).
Ceiling (plate 87).

TREVISO

PINACOTECA
Portrait of a Dominican Steward (plates 111–12).

CHURCH OF SAN NICCOLÒ
Heralds on the Onigo Monument (plates 212–13; attribution).

CHURCH OF SANTA CRISTINA AL TIVARONE
The Dead Saviour (Plate 12a).
The Santa Cristina Altarpiece (plates 12–15).

VENICE

CHURCH OF THE CARMINI
St Nicholas of Bari in Glory (plates 133–34).

CINI COLLECTION
Portrait of a Gentleman (plate 167).

PRIVATE COLLECTION
St Jerome in the Wilderness (plate 164b).

GALLERIE DELL'ACCADEMIA
Young Man in His Study (plates 126–28).

MUSEO CORRER
Madonna Nursing the Christ Child (plate 104).
Portrait of a Man Wearing a Red Cap (plate 210; attribution).

CHURCH OF SAN GIACOMO DELL'ORIO
Madonna Enthrone with Four Saints (plate 191).

BASILICA OF SAN MARCO
St Mark in Prayer (plate 194).

CHURCH OF SAN GIOVANNI E PAOLO
St Antoninus Altarpiece (plates 175–78).

VIENNA

KUNSTHISTORISCHES MUSEUM
Bust of a Youth Against a White Curtain (plate 16).
A Dominican Saint Preaching (plate 25).
Gentleman Holding a Golden Claw (plate 125).
Sacra Conversazione (plate 131).
Portrait of a Man in Three Positions (plate 135).
Christ in Glory with the Symbols of the Passion (plate 187).

WASHINGTON (DISTRICT OF COLUMBIA)

NATIONAL GALLERY OF ART (S. H. Kress Collection)
Allegorical Scene (plate 4).
A Maiden's Dream (plate 5).
St Catherine of Alexandria (plate 62).
The Nativity (plate 63).

WILTON HOUSE (SALISBURY)

EARL OF PEMBROKE COLLECTION
St Anthony the Hermit (plate 164a).

BIBLIOGRAPHICAL NOTE

We limit ourselves to pointing out the works directly concerning Lorenzo Lotto and his art.

G. VASARI. *Le Vite*, edited by C. L. Ragghianti, Milan, 1947.

F. M. TASSI. *Vite dei Pittore, Scultori e Architetti Bergamaschi*, Bergamo, 1793.

P. LOCATELLI. *Illustri Bergamaschi*, I, Bergamo, 1867.

H. VON TSCHUDI. "Lorenzo Lotto in den Marcken," in *Repertorium für Kunstwissenschaft*, 1887.

G. BAMPO. "Spigolature nell'Archivio Notarile di Treviso," in *Archivio Veneto*, 1886.

B. CECCHETTI. "Il testamento di Lorenzo Lotto," in *Archivio Veneto*, 1887.

G. MORELLI. *Italian Painters*, V. I and II, London, 1892–93.

P. GIANUIZZI. "Lorenzo Lotto e le sue opere nelle Marche," in *Nuova Rivista Misena*, 1894.

B. BERENSON. *Lorenzo Lotto*, London 1895 (Second edition, 1905; Third edition, Milan, 1955).

A. VENTURI. "Il 'Libro dei conti' di Lorenzo Lotto," in *Gallerie Nazionali Italiane*, I, 1895.

G. FRIZZONI. "Lorenzo Lotto pittore," in *Archivio storico dell'arte*, 1895 (Reviewed by Berenson).

G. BISCARO. "Lorenzo Lotto a Treviso," in *L'Arte*, 1898 and 1901.

CROWE and CAVALCASELLE. *History of Painting in North Italy*, Third edition edited by T. Borenius, London, 1912.

R. LONGHI. "Quesiti carvaggeschi," in *Pinacotheca*, 1928.

A. PINETTI. "Cronistoria artistica di Lorenzo Lotto di S. Maria Maggiore: V—Il coro ligneo di G. F. Capoferri e i disegni di Lorenzo Lotto per le tarsie," in *Bergomum*, 1928.

A. VENTURI. *Storia dell'arte italiana*, IX, iv, Milan, 1929.

E. VON DEN BERCKEN. "Lorenzo Lotto," in Thieme-Becker, *Kunstliches Lexikon*, 1929.

L. BIAGI. *Lorenzo Lotto*, Rome, 1942.

R. PALLUCCHINI. *La pittura veneziana del Cinquecento*, I, Novara, 1944.

H. and E. TIETZE. *The Drawings of the Venetian Painters*, New York, 1944.

R. LONGHI. *Viatico per cinque secoli di pittura veneziana*, Florence, 1946.

A. BANTI. *Lorenzo Lotto*, Florence 1955 (with chronology, notes and catalogue by A. Boschetto).

T. PIGNATTI. *Lorenzo Lotto*, Milan, 1953.

L. COLETTI. *Lorenzo Lotto*, Bergamo, 1953.

C. ANGELINI. *Gli affreschi di Lorenzo Lotto in Bergamo*, Bergamo, 1953.

Mostra di Lorenzo Lotto. Official catalogue edited by P. Zampetti, Venice, 1953.

P. ZAMPETTI. "Un capolavoro del Lotto ritrovato," in *Arte Veneta*, 1957.

H. S. FRANCIS. "Portraits by Lorenzo Lotto," in *The Bulletin of the Cleveland Museum of Art*, March 1957.

A. SPAHN. "Zur Lorenzo Lotto Literatur," in *Kunstkronik*, n. 4, 1960.

REPRODUCTIONS

ACKNOWLEDGEMENT
FOR PLATES

Fiorentini, Venice: plates 1A, 2, 3, 6–11, 16–24, 27A, 27B, 28, 31, 32B, 33B, 35A, 38–42, 45–47, 50, 51, 53, 55–59, 61, 64–68, 105, 106, 108, 110, 115–130, 132–135, 137–141, 144, 145A, 146, 148–150, 154–162, 164B, 169, 174, 175, 177, 178, 180–184, 186, 191, 193, 195, 196, 206–211, 216; *A.F.I., Venice:* plates 12–15, 104, 107A, 107B, 109, 111, 112, 145B, 151, 170–173, 176, 212A, 212B, 213A, 213B; *Da Re, Bergamo:* plates 73–103; *Alinari, Florence:* plates 29, 48B, 52, 142, 153, 163, 179, 189, 202, 203; *Anderson, Rome:* plates 36, 37, 69, 166, 190, 204; *Gabinetto Fotografico Nazionale, Rome:* plates 201, 205; *Perotti, Milan:* plates 54, 147; *Wolfrum, Vienna:* plates 25, 131; *Studio dell'illustrazione, Milan:* plate 192; *Burnell, Sarasota:* plate 165; plates 4, 5, 26A, 35B, 44, 60, 62, 63, 71, 72, 114, 136, 152A, 152B, 188, 197, 215A, 215B, 215C *are reproduced by courtesy of the respective galleries.*

Plate 94a. THE CREDARO FRESCOES: GOD THE FATHER
Credaro (Bergamo), Church of San Giorgio

Plate 94b. THE CREDARO FRESCOES: ST GEORGE SLAYING
THE DRAGON
Credaro (Bergamo), Church of San Giorgio

Plate 95. THE CREDARO FRESCOES: THE NATIVITY WITH SS ROCK
AND SEBASTIAN
Credaro (Bergamo), Church of San Giorgio

Plate 96. THE CREDARO FRESCOES: SS JEROME AND ANTHONY OF
PADUA and ST LAWRENCE
Credaro (Bergamo), Church of San Giorgio

Plate 97. THE CREDARO FRESCOES: SS BARTHOLOMEW AND CATHERINE
OF ALEXANDRIA and ST GEORGE
Credaro (Bergamo), Church of San Giorgio

Plate 98. GOD THE FATHER SUPPORTED BY ANGELS
Bergamo, Church of San Michele al Pozzo Bianco

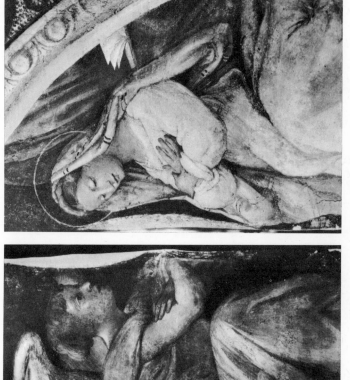

Plate 99. THE ANNUNCIATION
Bergamo, Church of San Michele al Pozzo Bianco

Plate 100. THE BIRTH OF THE VIRGIN
Bergamo, Church of San Michele at Pozzo Bianco

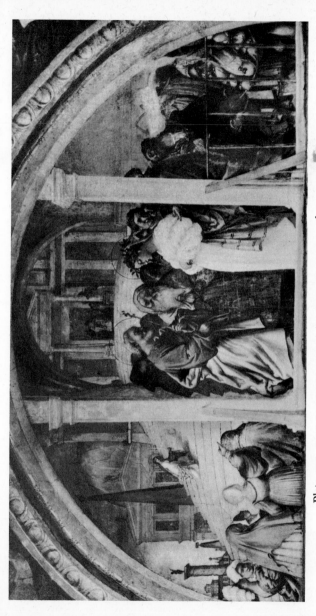

Plate 101. THE PRESENTATION IN THE TEMPLE and THE MARRIAGE
OF THE VIRGIN
Bergamo, Church of San Michele al Pozzo Bianco

Plate 102. *Detail of plate 100*

Plate 103. THE VISITATION
Bergamo, Church of San Michele al Pozzo Bianco

Plate 104. MADONNA NURSING THE CHRIST CHILD
Venice, Museo Correr

Plate 105. PORTRAIT OF AN ARCHITECT
Berlin, Staatliches Museen

Plate 106. PORTRAIT OF A YOUTH AGAINST A GREEN CURTAIN
Berlin, Staatliches Museen

Plate 107. SS FRANCIS AND CLARE, Jesi, Pinacoteca
MADONNA ENTHRONED WITH SAINTS, Jesi, Pinacoteca

Plate 108. THE ARCHANGEL GABRIEL
Jesi, Pinacoteca

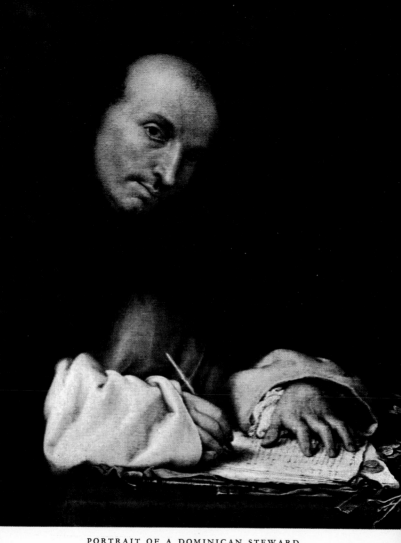

PORTRAIT OF A DOMINICAN STEWARD
Treviso, Pinacoteca
(*detail of plate III*)

Plate 109. THE ANNUNCIATE VIRGIN
Jesi, Pinacoteca

Plate 110. PORTRAIT OF A YOUNG MAN
Milan, Castello Sforzesco

Plate III. PORTRAIT OF A DOMINICAN STEWARD
Treviso, Pinacoteca

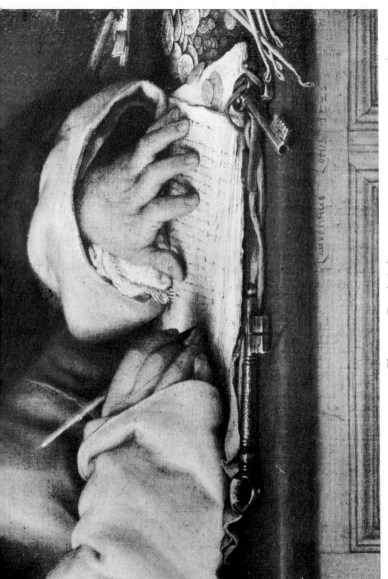

Plate 112. *Detail of plate 111*

Plate 113; MADONNA IN LANDSCAPE WITH TWO DONORS
formerly New York, W. R. Hearst Collection

Plate 114. BUST OF A YOUTH AGAINST A RED CURTAIN
Berlin, Staatliches Museen

Plate 115. THE ASSUMPTION OF THE VIRGIN
Celana (Bergamo), Church of Santa Maria Assunta

Plate 116. THE PONTERANICA POLYPTYCH: ST PETER and THE
REDEEMER
Ponteranica (Bergamo), Church of Santi Vincenzo e Alessandro

Plate 117. THE PONTERANICA POLYPTYCH: ST JOHN THE BAPTIST
and ST PAUL
Ponteranica (Bergamo), Church of Santi Vincenzo e Alessandro

Plate 118. THE PONTERANICA POLYPTYCH: THE ARCHANGEL GABRIEL
Ponteranica (Bergamo), Church of Santi Vincenzo e Alessandro

Plate 119. THE PONTERANICA POLYPTYCH: THE ANNUNCIATE VIRGIN
Ponteranica (Bergamo), Church of Santi Vincenzo e Alessandro

Plate 120. THE NATIVITY
Siena, Pinacoteca

Plate 121. MAN ON A TERRACE
Cleveland (Ohio), Museum of Art

Plate 122. PORTRAIT OF BISHOP TOMMASO NEGRI
Split, Monastero delle Paludi

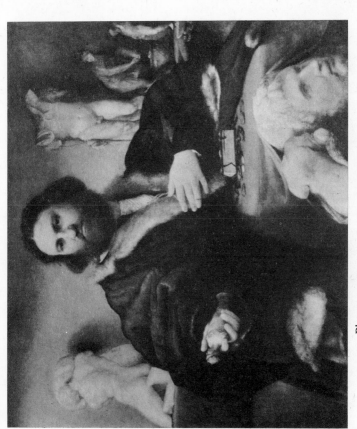

Plate 123, PORTRAIT OF ANDREA ODONI
Hampton Court, Royal Gallery

Plate 124. *Detail of plate 123*

THE NATIVITY
Siena, Pinacoteca
(*detail of plate 120*)

Plate 125. GENTLEMAN HOLDING A GOLDEN CLAW
Vienna, Kunsthistorisches Museum

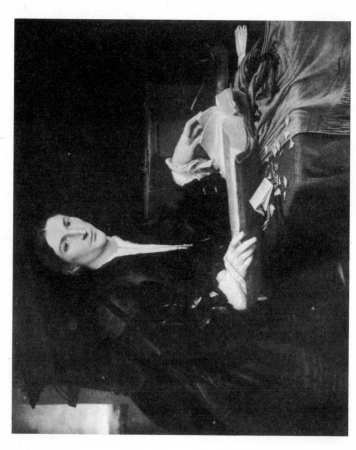

Plate 126. YOUNG MAN IN HIS STUDY
Venice, Gallerie dell'Accademia

Plate 127. *Detail of plate 126*

Plate 128. *Detail of plate 126*

Plate 129. THE ADORATION OF THE SHEPHERDS
Brescia, Pinacoteca Tosio-Martinengo

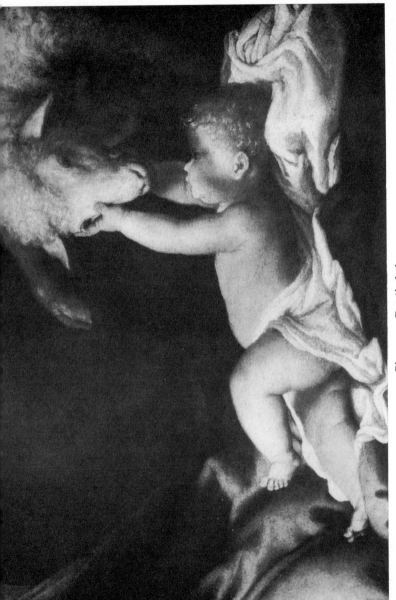

Plate 130. *Detail of plate 129*

Plate 131. SACRA CONVERSAZIONE
Vienna, Kunsthistorisches Museum

Plate 132. THE ANNUNCIATION
Recanati, Church of Santa Maria sopra Mercanti

Plate 133. ST NICHOLAS OF BARI IN GLORY
Venice, Church of the Carmini

Plate 134. *Detail of plate 133*

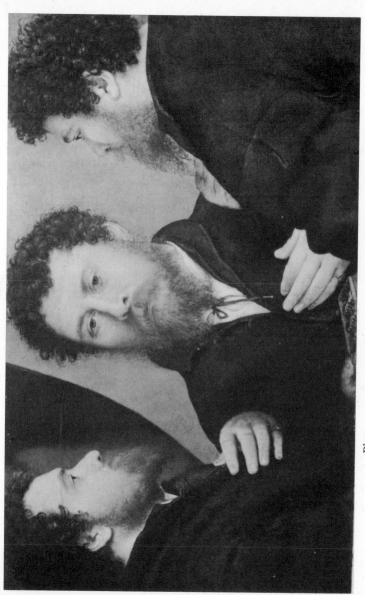

Plate 135. PORTRAIT OF A MAN IN THREE POSITIONS
Vienna, Kunsthistorisches Museum

Plate 136. PORTRAIT OF A LADY AS LUCRETIA
London, National Gallery

Plate 137. THE ALLEGORY OF CHASTITY
Rome, Rospigliosi-Pallavicini Collection

Plate 138. *Detail of plate 137*

Plate 139. PORTRAIT OF A GENTLEMAN DRESSED IN BLACK
Rome, Borghese Gallery

Plate 140. *Detail of plate 139*

Plate 141. *Detail of plate 139*

Plate 142. CHRIST AND THE ADULTERESS
Paris, Louvre

Plate 143. APOLLO ASLEEP ON PARNASSUS
Budapest, Museum of Fine Arts

Plate 144. MALE PORTRAIT
Milan, Crespi Collection

Plate 145. THE ANNUNCIATION and THE VISITATION
Jesi, Pinacoteca

Plate 146. *Detail of plate 145*

Plate 147. CHRIST ON THE CROSS WITH THE SYMBOLS OF THE
PASSION
Florence, Berenson Collection

Plate 148. THE CRUCIFIXION
Monte San Giusto (Macerata), Church of Santa Maria in Telusiano

Plate 149. *Detail of plate 148*

Plate 150. *Detail of plate 148*

Plate 151. *Detail of plate 148*

Plate 152. ST SEBASTIAN and ST CHRISTOPHER
Berlin, Staatliches Museen

Plate 153. SS ROCK, CHRISTOPHER, AND SEBASTIAN
Loreto, Palazzo Apostolico

Plate 154. THE ST LUCY ALTARPIECE
Jesi, Pinacoteca

Plate 155. *Detail of plate 154*

Plate 156. SCENES FROM THE LEGEND OF ST LUCY
Jesi, Pinacoteca

Plate 157. SCENES FROM THE LEGEND OF ST LUCY
Jesi, Pinacoteca

Plate 158. SCENES FROM THE LEGEND OF ST LUCY
Jesi, Pinacoteca

Plate 159. Details of plates 156 and 158

Plate 160. PORTRAIT OF A GENTLEMAN
New Orleans, Delgado Museum of Art

Plate 161. HOLY FAMILY WITH ST CATHERINE
Bergamo, Accademia Carrara

Plate 162. VIRGIN AND CHILD WITH SS ANNE, JOACHIM, AND JEROME
Florence, Uffizi

Plate 163. THE RECOGNITION OF THE HOLY CHILD
Paris, Louvre

Plate 164. ST ANTHONY THE HERMIT, Wilton House
ST JEROME IN THE WILDERNESS, Venice

Plate 165. MADONNA WITH SLEEPING CHILD
Sarasota (Florida), Ringling Museum of Art

Plate 166. PORTRAIT OF A MAN AGED THIRTY-SEVEN
Rome, Doria Gallery

Plate 167. PORTRAIT OF A GENTLEMAN
Venice, Cini Collection

Plate 168. THE RECOGNITION OF THE HOLY CHILD
formerly in the Town Hall at Osimo

Plate 169. THE MADONNA OF THE ROSARY
Cingoli (Macerata), Church of San Domenico

Plate 170. *Detail of plate 169*

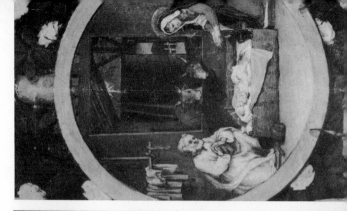

Plate 171. *Details of plate 169*

Plate 172. *Details of plate 169*

PORTRAIT OF LAURA DA POLA
Milan, Brera Gallery
(detail of plate 183)

Plate 173. *Details of plate 169*

Plate 174. MADONNA ENTHRONED WITH FOUR SAINTS
Ancona, Church of Santa Maria della Piazza

Plate 175. ST ANTONINUS ALTARPIECE
Venice, Church of San Giovanni e Paolo

Plate 176. *Detail of plate 175*

Plate 177. *Detail of plate 175*

Plate 178. *Detail of plate 175*

Plate 179. ST JEROME IN THE WILDERNESS
Rome, Doria Gallery

Plate 180. VIRGIN IN GLORY WITH SAINTS
Sedrina (Bergamo), Parish Church

Plate 181. ST FELIX
Giovanazzo (Bari), Church of San Domenico

Plate 182. PORTRAIT OF MESSER FEBO DA BRESCIA
Milan, Brera Gallery

Plate 183. PORTRAIT OF LAURA DA POLA
Milan, Brera Gallery

Plate 184. PORTRAIT OF AN OLD MAN
Milan, Brera Gallery

Plate 185. PORTRAIT OF A MAN WITH SYMBOLS
El Paso (Texas), Museum of Art

Plate 186. PORTRAIT OF AN ELDERLY GENTLEMAN
Milan, Brera Gallery

Plate 187. CHRIST IN GLORY WITH THE SYMBOLS OF THE PASSION
Vienna, Kunsthistorisches Museum

Plate 188. PORTRAIT OF THE SURGEON STUER WITH HIS SON
Philadelphia, J. G. Johnson Collection

ST JEROME IN THE WILDERNESS
Madrid, Prado
(*detail of plate 190*)

Plate 189. PIETÀ
Milan, Brera Gallery

Plate 190. ST JEROME IN THE WILDERNESS
Madrid, Prado

Plate 191. MADONNA ENTHRONED WITH FOUR SAINTS
Venice, Church of San Giacomo dell'Orio

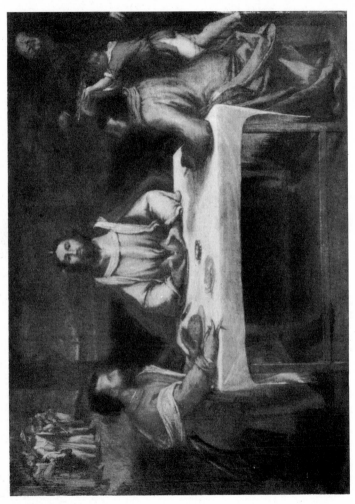

Plate 192. CHRIST AT EMMAUS
Oxford, Christ Church Library

Plate 193. VIRGIN AND CHILD WITH ZACHARIAS AND ST JOHN
THE BAPTIST
Milan, Poldi-Pezzoli Museum

M·D·XLV

VBI DILIGENTER INSPEXERIS, ARTEMQVE AC LABOREM
FRANCISCI ET VALERII ZVCATI VENETOR. FRATRVM
AGNOVERIS, TVM DEMVM IVDICATO

Plate 194. ST MARK IN PRAYER
Venice, Atrium of San Marco

Plate 195. PORTRAIT OF A DOMINICAN FRIAR AS ST PETER MARTYR
Cambridge (Massachusetts), Fogg Art Museum

Plate 196. MADONNA IN GLORY WITH SAINTS
Mogliano (Macerata), Parish Church

Plate 197. THE ASSUMPTION OF THE VIRGIN
Ancona, Pinacoteca

Plate 198. THE RETURN OF THE PRODIGAL SON
Florence, Private Collection

Plate 199. THE ENTOMBMENT
Florence, Private Collection

Plate 200. MAN WITH AN ARQUEBUS
Rome, Pinacoteca Capitolina

Plate 201. THE BAPTISM OF CHRIST
Loreto, Palazzo Apostolico

Plate 202. THE SACRIFICE OF MELCHIZEDEK
Loreto, Palazzo Apostolico

Plate 203. THE RECOGNITION OF THE HOLY CHILD
Loreto, Palazzo Apostolico

Plate 204. ST MICHAEL DRIVING LUCIFER OUT OF HEAVEN
Loreto, Palazzo Apostolico

Plate 205. THE ADORATION OF THE MAGI
Loreto, Palazzo Apostolico

Plate 206. THE PRESENTATION IN THE TEMPLE
Loreto, Palazzo Apostolico

Plate 207. *Detail of plate 206*

Plate 208. *Detail of plate 206*

Plate 209. THE TOILET OF VENUS
Milan, Private Collection

ATTRIBUTED PAINTINGS

Plate 210. PORTRAIT OF A MAN WEARING A RED CAP
Venice, Museo Correr (*attrib.*)

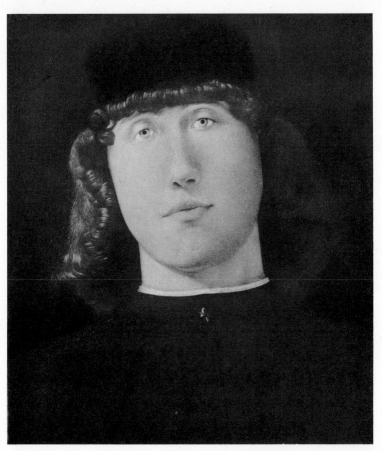

Plate 211. PORTRAIT OF A YOUTH
Bergamo, Accademia Carrara (*attrib.*)

Plate 212. HERALDS ON THE ONIGO MONUMENT
Treviso, Church of San Niccolò (*attrib.*)

Plate 213. *Details of plate 212*

Plate 214. DEAD CHRIST IN LANDSCAPE
Asolo, Parish Church (*attrib.*)

Plate 215. SKETCHES FROM THE LEGEND OF ST STEPHEN
Bergamo, Accademia Carrara (*attrib.*)

Plate 216. CHRIST LEAVING THE HALL OF JUDGMENT
Milan, Private Collection (*attrib.*)